Angela Goode, co-author of *Great Working Dog Stories*, published in 1990, has been a rural columnist since 1981. Her columns have appeared in *The Advertiser* in Adelaide, *The Weekly Times* Victoria, and broadcast on the ABC's South Australian Country Hour, where *Great Working Dog Stories* had its genesis.

Before she left the city for farming, Angela Goode was a radio copywriter, television presenter and a journalist at *The Advertiser*.

MORE GREAT WORKING DOG STORIES

A National tribute to Australian working dogs
by those who work with them

Edited and compiled by
ANGELA GOODE

Illustrated by Jennifer Barnett

an
ABC
BOOK

Published by ABC Books for the
AUSTRALIAN BROADCASTING CORPORATION
GPO Box 9994 Sydney NSW 2001

First published November, 1992
Reprinted December 1992 (Twice)
Reprinted February 1993
Reprinted December 1993
Reprinted May 1995

National Library of Australia
Cataloguing-in-Publication entry
More great working dog stories.
    ISBN 0 7333 0260 2.
    1. Working dogs—Australia—Anecdotes.
    I. Goode, Angela. II. Australian Broadcasting Corporation.
    III. Title: Australia all over (Radio program).

636.73

Illustrated by Jennifer Barnett
Edited by Jo Jarrah
Designed by Helen Semmler
Set in 9½/12pt Schneidler Old Style by Midland Typesetters
    Maryborough, Victoria
Printed and bound in Australia by Australian Print Group
    Maryborough, Victoria

1695-7-5-3-3-3-3-3

10 9 8 7 6

FOREWORD

Working farm dogs are regarded by many as the only *real* dogs—not the pampered wimps sometimes found nursing their hypochondria in suburban backyards. Tough like their owners, they are kept not for their good looks, just for their talent in helping produce the nation's export wool and meat income.

Outside a pub after a hard day in the sale yards, a heap of muddy utes will be parked in untidy rows under the straggly gums and pepper trees. While their drivers wash away the dirt and manure with a few jugs, the dogs outside will be peeing on each other's ute wheels, having the odd fight or sexual conquest, sleeping or fending off canine trespassers with a heck of a lot of barking. Inside, the human behaviour will be pretty similar, figuratively speaking. More than likely, there'll be some serious one-upmanship in boasting about their dogs.

This book attempts to snare the stories about the great dogs, the memorable dogs and the hilarious incidents that people often first share over a few drinks, or at the kitchen table. The dogs within have been paid the supreme compliment by their owners who in typical stoic bush style generally avoid getting carried away by too much sloppy sentimentalism.

For all their heroics and charm, working dogs after all are but working units on farms, which in the past few years have had to be ruthlessly pragmatic about freeloaders in an effort to stay afloat.

What started off some years ago as a nice idea to pay tribute to working dogs has evolved somewhat. So popular was the 1990 collection of stories from mainly South Australian farm people about their workmates, that Ian Doyle, executive producer Rural Radio South Australia and I issued in March this year an Australia-wide invitation for stories so the tribute to working dogs could be truly national. Almost 2000 stories were received.

No longer can we say Australian working dogs are the unsung heroes of the bush. It seems they are now so well sung, they are in danger of getting swollen heads. Next, they'll be wanting carpet in their 44s and a couple of days off a week.

That only 145 of these stories can be fitted between the covers of this book is a tragedy. Hundreds of equally marvellous stories have had to be left out with heart-wrenching reluctance. As I re-read many times those on my 'short' list of 390, the one consoling thought was that there was indeed enough wonderful material for yet another book—so who knows?

It must also be said that all other types of working dogs such as drug sniffer dogs, guard dogs, hearing dogs, guide dogs, circus dogs and tracker dogs have been shamelessly discriminated against. Their work is no less valuable, nor are their talents less. Our focus, however, for the purposes of this book was specifically on farm dogs.

There's always a risk when making a blanket call for stories that the response will be unbalanced or narrow in range. However as bag after bag of stories reached me, I could only rejoice in their scope. My task became one of determining what elements of dogs' lives would be explored in the book. Early in the project I constructed a chapter plan and loosely matched stories to it in order to be sure of achieving a book that had form despite having been written by 140 different people.

The result is much more than a eulogy to working dogs. The book is just as much an account of the lives of rural people through the seasons, highs and lows of the bush from the time the first working dogs were imported into Victoria from Scotland in 1869.

The stories take you back into history, to the early droving days, when bullocks strained at their yokes and before the noise of civilization interrupted the dialogue between dogs and workers. Bryan Bowman in 'The Dogs of Old Glen Helen' reckons today's dogs are soft because they spend too much time in utes and on bikes. A close rapport is also hard to build when you have to shout at the dog over the sound of a noisy engine. The old timers say they had some truly great dogs when they did all their work on horse and foot, and had hours to yarn and teach them the ropes in a gentle relaxed way. The inevitable question is—Have we seen the last of the truly great dogs? Many, like Lyndon Cooper, 'Nacooma Gus— A Legend in his Own Lifetime' will vehemently disagree.

A woman's place on a farm was said traditionally to be five paces behind the working dog. This sorry state of affairs is still so— certainly in the eyes of a few dogs! Heather Edwards, 'I'm not your Bloody Dog' and Marj Wood, 'I Should Bloody Well Think So' put the victimised woman's view.

Inevitably, the sense of despair felt on most farms in the past few years following droughts and the collapse of the wool price can be detected in many stories. Accounts of the '30s Depression, when dogs worked as rabbiters and 'roo killers, further remind us of the fragile changeability of fortunes on the land. Always, though, when things seem at their blackest, a dog will nudge comfortingly closer as you stand yarning about the miseries of life with a neighbour at the mailbox; or guided by extraordinary telepathy from beyond, will lift his leg on the trouser of unwelcome visitors like salesmen and bank managers.

The bond welded between work mates after years of toil together and the pain of parting is poignantly described by Geoffrey Blight in 'Father's Day'.

I extend my gratitude to all those who wrote stories and for giving me so much pleasure reading them. I congratulate every one of them. It's not always easy to take time out of a busy farm day to sit down and write a story—but that so many did and produced such natural, spontaneous stories indicates that rural people perpetuate the art and great traditions of story telling.

For prizes of a year's supply of dog food and $250 vouchers from the ABC shop, we judged Ron Kerr's story 'Sandsoap' to be the winner of the serious section, and Greg Standfield's story 'Stretch Goes to the Big Smoke' winner of the humorous section.

The judging ordeal was shared with Lyndon Cooper, the current holder of the South Australian Yard Dog Championship title, Dr Robert Holmes, veterinarian and animal behaviourist, Armadale, Victoria, and Ian Doyle. I thank them all for their wise, caring consideration of the finalists.

The tireless Ian, doing his best to emulate a frenetic, workaholic kelpie, also handled radio promotions and the production of the 'More Great Working Dog Stories' audio tape.

For the two dog food prizes of 800 kilograms of Meaty Bites and help with the book's launch we thank Uncle Ben's of Australia. Other thanks go to the many neighbouring farmers, dog breeders and dog triallers who helped me with terminology, information and advice—in particular Nancy Withers, president of the South Australian Yard Dog Association.

The stories, according to the brief set by us, had to be true. I have spoken to a great many of the writers to clarify details during the editing process and it seems this criterion was carefully observed. The stories are all the stronger for it.

Finally, at a time when the pain of unemployment is being felt through city and country, the stories above all celebrate the joys to be found in work. The delight on the face of a dog as it jumps on to the back of the ute to go off on a day's mustering should be able to be worn on the faces of more people in this nation.

Angela Goode

CONTENTS

HISTORY OF THE KELPIE

Olive Hargrave, Yarrawonga, Victoria

In about 1869, John Rutherford, a highly respected pastoral pioneer and Yarrawonga identity, was sent a pair of top breeding dogs by his brother who lived at Dunrobin, Sutherlandshire, in Scotland.

The working ability of the Scottish dogs with sheep was excellent, but they were poorly equipped to handle the harsh conditions of the colony. So John Rutherford, who lived at Yarrawonga Station and was a fine judge of animals, set about improving the breed.

From the Scottish dogs, Rutherford bred Moss, a smooth-haired, prick-eared black dog with a splash of white on his neck. Moss is regarded as the grand-sire of the kelpie breed.

In 1869, another grazier, George Robertson of Warrock Station near Casterton in Victoria, imported another pair of breeding dogs from Scotland.

From his breeding program, he produced a bitch which was later to be called Gleeson's Kelpie after Jack Gleeson of Murray Downs Station, Victoria, who acquired her in exchange for his horse.

Jack Gleeson named the bitch Kelpie after the mythical Scottish spirit that was supposed to frequent fiords and rivers on stormy nights, and make itself apparent to those about to drown. Usually appearing in the form of a horse, the spirit itself was sometimes regarded as harmful.

Messrs Elliot and Allen of Geraldra Station imported yet another pair of dogs from Scotland in 1870. Mr Elliot was a brother-in-law of George Robertson of Warrock Station. The dogs were named Brutus and Jenny, and their matings produced Caesar, Laddie and Nero. A mating of Caesar to Gleeson's Kelpie produced a bitch called King's Kelpie. Moss was mated several times to Gleeson's Kelpie and King's Kelpie. It is now generally considered that it was from these matings that the cross was established from which all good kelpies evolved.

Laddie was mated with King's Kelpie and produced Sally. Moss was mated with Sally and a pup from the litter, a jet black, prick-eared, smooth-coated dog like its father, was given to a station hand named Jack Davis. He named his pup Barb after Barb, the hardy black racehorse of African descent that won the Melbourne Cup in 1866.

One of the pups from a mating of Moss and King's Kelpie was Clyde. When Clyde was mated with one of Walter King's bitches named Gary, the litter produced what many consider to be the best working dog of all time, a dog named Coil.

In the Sydney sheepdog trials of 1898, Coil was worked by Jack Quin and in the preliminary trial scored full points from a possible 100.

That evening, he was run over by a cab and suffered a broken leg. The next day, Coil went into the finals with his broken leg hanging loose and, again, was awarded a perfect score. This feat has never been equalled.

The world's first sheepdog trials are believed to have been held at Forbes, New South Wales, in about 1871 or 1872. The winner was a bitch named Kelpie, daughter of another bitch imported from Scotland.

Yarrawonga has every reason to be proud of its heritage as the birthplace of the kelpie breed, through Moss, one of its most famous sons—the first link in the breeding chain of Australian working kelpies and barbs.

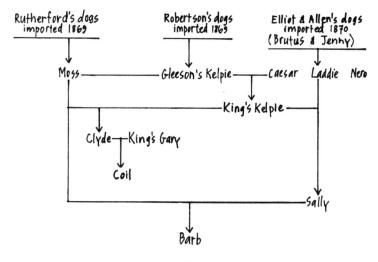

GETTING ACQUAINTED

Geraldine Boylan, Port Lincoln, South Australia

Between 1988 and 1991 I worked as a counsellor with rural communities. Having been raised as farm girl I was well versed with the position held by the farm dog on the farm. To my joy I found nothing had changed over time. Traditions reigned supreme, or should I say the place held by the farm dog did.

I quickly recaptured my former knowledge and set about to put it into practice. To give the dog his or her rightful place—he or she runs the farm and knows everything about everything that goes on, and if you make it with them then you have made it for life.

On arrival at a farm I developed the habit of winding down my car window and spending time quietly getting acquainted with the 'Boss' of the farm or with the 'Boss and his or her supporters'. They never let me down. They always rolled up to give me the once-over.

I learned much from observing these dogs. Sometimes I established a relationship quickly. A few words had them literally eating from my hand. At other times the inspection was more comprehensive—the wheels received the usual 'sniff and wee' treatment before I was given so much as a stare. Once the look in their eyes went from watchful to mellow, I learned to open the door and to sit quietly and allow the personal inspection. Mostly I found that after sniffs and a few licks, I'd made the grade.

After a while I learned to place the dogs in three categories—the wary, the smoochers and the rude. The wary dog often remained aloof, watchful and tense until I earned his acceptance. Thank goodness this type was scarce. At times I looked for a correlation between the tenseness of the dog and the tension on the home front, but I found no support for this notion.

With quiet talking the reserved dog could eventually be won over. I remember one occasion when I sat in the car and calmly explained the purpose of my visit to the dog; I explained I was the 'good guy'.

I was not the bank manager. At that moment a head came around the shed corner and a voice said, 'I'm glad about that. I wasn't coming out—until I heard you say that.'

The smoochers were pushover dogs. Thank goodness they were in plentiful supply. My affairs with them were mutually satisfying.

To explain the third category I need to tell a story. One day I called at a farm and as I went through my usual performance a young pre-school lass came and swung on the house garden gate. Immediately she joined the conversation, giving a rundown on the dogs together with some strong advice.

'Watch out for Brucey. He's rude.'

Ignoring the dogs, I climbed from the car to join the child. Just then this dog thrust his head between my legs.

'See, I told you to watch him. He's rude.'

During the three years, I found many such dogs. Indeed there were more rude dogs on farms than any other types. They seemed to take great delight in actions which defied all words and which rendered unexpected and immediate embarrassment.

But in a way I respected these rude dogs. Their instincts still ruled supreme despite their training and complex skills. Even though they were totally obedient and submissive to a boss in the paddock, they were still masters of themselves. Politeness, the mark of civilised society, could never be trained into these dogs. They had everyone at their mercy. Any visitor with a superior air and an expensive suit could be humbled with a good sniff in the crutch.

Throughout the three years I never ceased to be in awe of the knowledge, and the silent stories, that were communicated through the farm dogs' eyes.

The dogs often made it clear what was going on, what was the state of the bank balance, how depressed were their owners. If a farm was falling to pieces you'd often find half a dead sheep dragged on to the verandah, holes dug all around the house and dogs and their mess lying around everywhere. There'd be a general air of decay as the dogs extended their territory into that of their owners who no longer were able to take an interest in disciplining their dogs and drawing boundaries between dog and human.

You could see loneliness in the eyes of these dogs. They were no longer working—all the stock had gone. They were starved for company as the wives were out working and the kids had left home to look for work in the city.

There was an air of resignation in a lot of these dogs' eyes. They'd throw themselves at you with a sort of desperate joyfulness, happy to have company, but looking for leadership and purpose once more to their lives.

PART 1

TRIBUTES

· *Paying respect*
· *An insight into the life of a working dog*
· *The value of a good dog*
· *Their work*

TOUGH COUNTRY, TOUGH DOGS

Peter Clarke, Kununurra, Western Australia

I used to work as overseer on Tubbo Station in the New South Wales Riverina. Tubbo was a sheepdog's paradise with up to 35,000 merino sheep of fine quality.

There were good-sized paddocks for the dogs to have a decent cast around, big yards, big numbers and big mobs. Struth, the Tubbo woolshed is 102 stands and to fill her up with 3,000 woolly sheep, good dogs were needed. Many a time I saw old Bob's dog Humphrey back a running mob of wethers 200 yards up through the yards and way through the shed, turn round and back them in the other direction as they ran in.

Sheepdogs! The outstation overseer ran anywhere between fourteen and nineteen dogs at once. His ute was a mobile dog kennel and butchery, with kelpies, border collie crosses and the odd collie thrown in—all different sizes, different ages, and different levels of ability.

The ute sides were strung with roo legs and old sheep that made up the tucker for these dogs. His job involved a lot of droving and mustering of lines of sheep of similar age from various paddocks into one mob and taking them the 30 miles into the shed. Mobs of 4,000 were common and even bigger mobs of 12,000 weaners were handled by dogs on Tubbo.

It is a skilful team of man and dog that can count through a gate 3,000 to 4,000 sheep, keep tallies, direct the odd young dog and keep the ants out of one's boots all at once.

A dog is a man's best friend. My top dog was a kelpie-New Zealand border collie bitch called Lucy. Sheep were her life. In winter when the ice was on the puddles, she'd have a good swim, then jump up on the ute ready for work.

She would sit on a whistle or wave of a hand away across the paddock. She would work on a wing or tail a mob for miles with no directions. She worked on when her body wanted to stop—130

3

degrees or more in the sun, pads worn and cracked and troughs miles apart, but she never let me down. Never. She was my friend and my helper. I couldn't have done the job with only my four dogs if Lucy wasn't there. A dog is worth five men and Lucy worth five dogs.

I told her through a veil of tears how much I loved her as I buried her after a 'pig dog' fought her to death. My wife and I were off the property and arrived home to be confronted with our best friend ripped to pieces.

When she needed me most I wasn't there but she was always there for me. I feel I let her down. That's what really hurts. She was killed three nights before we were due to move to Texas Downs where Lucy was going to retire, as no dogs were used there.

QUEENIE WITH THE DASHING TONGUE

Louella Vaughan, Mogilla, New South Wales

A droving friend of mine, Ted, had a red kelpie called Queenie. On quiet command she would be sent to turn the head or bring up the rear of the roving mobs.

In the full heat of summer, far from dams and creeks where cattle often break and run, I've seen Queenie work to hold the mob until she was staggering from thirst and exhaustion. Ted's hardy old Akubra would then quickly be adapted to make a water bowl to revive her.

At home after the evening meal was finished, a chair would sometimes be pulled up—'but not too near the table'—for Queenie. The mock kissing game which ensued would keep us all amused as the bespectacled, leathery face of the drover would tease his sleek, seal-like kelpie.

Her head would bow in false and knowing modesty, her eyes turned upward coyly at her owner, watching for that opportunity for her dashing tongue to make contact with the cheek that came so temptingly close, then jerked away. Affection masked by chastisement would follow: 'By Jesus, Queenzy, don't you go kissin' me.'

Her head would drop and the kelpie grin would turn to a Mona Lisa smile as she played the game over and over again and just now and then had a win, only to be called a 'dirty old thing'.

After the games, she'd be rewarded with a bone off a plate and would depart with a majestic air that indicated she really did understand the meaning of her name.

Somewhere in Queensland they took a mob. The day was hot, the grass was good and the herd had spread for what seemed like miles. Queenie was sent to bring the mob to check. She was on her way a 'long way back'. The rate of the dust rising from the road told Ted that a car was coming at a furious pace. He reckoned the driver would slow down when he realised the front stragglers were part of a mob. But he did not.

Too far away to warn Queenie, but close enough to witness the impact, Ted's heart missed a beat as he saw that she was hit. In rage he picked up a rock and hurled it at the passing car, shattering the windscreen. Still the driver did not bother to stop and Ted's curses were drowned out by the engine's roar.

Mounting his horse, he urged it through the settling dust to where Queenie lay.

'Sweet Jesus, why?' he whispered.

He took his pocket knife from its pouch and crouching over Queenie, slit her down the side. She had been heavily in pup and he thought one might just be alive.

The souped-up car and angry young driver returned with policeman in tow. The drover's weathered face was stony and white and the dust on it was wet and smeared from sweat—or tears.

In his trembling hands he still held the knife and in the other a fine, fat, lifeless pup, one from a litter of eight, their helpless bodies spread on the ground.

The copper cleared his throat and addressing the young driver said, 'Push off, son, you got off light. A bloke's dog out here's worth a man or three.'

And helplessly he stared at the scene of my friend, the still puppies and the corpse that was once our beautiful Queenie.

OWING A DEBT TO DOC

Geoffrey Blight, Narrogin, Western Australia

The day Charlie had to have Jenny put down was a bad day. The near sixteen year old bitch had slipped on the motorbike and mangled her legs. Charlie's son rushed her to the vet, then had to phone home and tell Charlie the worst possible news.

'Have him put her down,' was all Charlie said. The ageing sheep farmer sought the seclusion of the woodpile and for several hours moistened chips, remembering the years he'd spent with the old quarter-dingo kelpie-cross.

They'd shown them! On more than one occasion the extra-ordinarily tough old dog had shown what real dogs were made of. Never a sheep or other could call her bluff.

Even third prize in the State Yard Championship had dismayed the perfectionists, who had until then little time for the rough coated, often noisy dog that beat the living daylights out of any of their glamorous collies if they annoyed her. She always did things her way despite the loud protests from Charlie and threats to knock her bloody block off.

She'd had a good number of pups, some good, some a bit rough, but Charlie had kept a couple—Misty and Doc. Misty was good-looking, won a trial and was very obedient, but Doc was a bit too much like Jenny, hard to handle, wanting things his own way all the time, not to mention a bit rough on the sheep at times. He was inclined to give them something to remember if they didn't see it his way, but he was tougher than King Gees.

Charlie might not have kept him if he hadn't lost old Jenny and had a tragic poisoning of nearly all his dogs. So he was kind of stuck with Doc, if he wanted to keep the old part-dingo line of which he was so proud.

Doc was not just part-dingo, he looked and acted it—a big, funny kind of yellow-orange dog that prowled rather than ran. All Charlie's mates told him to get a better-bred dog and nearly succeeded when Charlie bought a very expensive but rather gutless border collie called Big Bob. Sure he worked trials well, but the bastard was useless at home. 'Weak as piss,' Charlie would say as an excuse to keep Doc to handle his 10,000 wild and woolly jumbucks.

When the wool prices collapsed in '89, Charlie's accountants told him to buy some cattle 'to balance things out'. Charlie got a herd of 30 Hereford-cross cows and calves. They were station bred, big wild buggers.

They may have been cheap for their size but they had rarely been handled, if at all, and were calving. Shifting them was nearly impossible. They went mad at dogs and a vehicle didn't do the job. Charlie found himself walking, leaving Doc, Big Bob and Misty on the ute, trying a bit of the old shoo shoo to get them out after they were delivered.

He thought he was going fine as he'd made it halfway across the paddock. He was at least twenty chain from the ute when a cow accidentally trod on a young calf belonging to a big, crumple-horned biddy of a cow, who immediately started to bellow and run around in a frenzy at the calling of the distressed calf.

Charlie had a weak heart. He'd been told many times to take things more easily and had been on medication for several years. When the big cow swung toward him, he was frightened. He couldn't run as there was nowhere to go. A second cow joined the act, threatening and running. Charlie couldn't turn around, or they'd have him. He roared and backed off hoping for something to defend himself with. There was nothing. More and more the cows stirred up, getting closer and closer to him. It was only a matter of time and he knew it.

A lot went through his mind in those seconds as she lined him up—desperation, fear, noise, as the whole herd psyched itself up. When she rushed, Charlie just shut his eyes, grimaced and hoped he could bear it.

The ground shook as she came the last few yards. Suddenly, over the bawling came an unexpected, deafening, howling bark. Charlie

7

only caught a glimpse of a leaping orange flash close by, being showered with dust and dung as the cow changed course to meet a much more threatening intruder.

When he looked, Doc had latched onto the nose of the cow and hung on. Charlie retreated. First slowly then, turning, weak heart or not, he half walked, half ran to the ute, knowing they still could get him if they wanted to. The noise told him the whole herd was joining in.

The cow swung Doc frantically to and fro trying to get him off, finally crashing him to the ground and rolling over him as he tried to take her with him. At last, the big cow bludgeoned Doc off, tossing him mercilessly skyward and charged again.

Doc, now badly injured, retreated slowly, barking and growling with every step. He bluffed to delay another charge. He could have escaped to the ute easily but he didn't. Legs broken, face badly damaged, cut and bruised, he stood his ground, letting Charlie, not game to look back, grasping his chest, finally make it to the ute. Big Bob sat staring at the action from the safety of the tray.

Exhausted, Charlie now looked back and saw the cows continuing their attack on the badly limping, still rebellious Doc. This motivated Charlie to start the ute and charge into the fray, separating the maddened cows from the bleeding, broken dog.

Charlie was born tough, had lived tough and there were rules. There is no room for crippled sheepdogs on farms. Therefore, you put them down. Charlie knew what the vet was going to say. He was ready for it. After all, it wasn't the first time. There had been Jenny, but she was old. Doc was only five.

Halfway to the vet's, he decided there was no harm in trying. Especially if it was only a couple of hundred dollars. He looked at the mutilated form breathing heavily on the seat, covered in blood, and wondered if two hundred would have been thought too much if it had been Charlie there—and it sure as hell could have been.

The vet looked at Charlie funnily, as if he had changed or something, when he found himself explaining how bad and expensive it was for so little chance of ever being right again. That is, if Doc even lived. The old man muttered something about owing the dog a chance. At this stage the vet was unaware of the morning's drama and Charlie sure didn't want to spend the rest of the day on the woodpile again.

Word gets around, especially if you're a popular bloke, and Charlie was one of those. After 24 hours, it was clear that Doc would survive though he'd be crippled. Charlie sat on his front porch as day broke, stroking the swollen, rugged head and plastered body and thanked his best friend for life. He wondered what it was that had brought Doc to his rescue and left the so-called 'good' dogs safe where they'd been told to sit.

His thoughts were interrupted when the noise of one, then two TV choppers came out of the gloom and settled in his front paddock. It would be a long day. There would be many more cars and crews wanting to know the secret of their bond. A bond only a few men have with their best friends.

Doc lives on, awarded the State's two highest bravery awards. No man is more proud of a crippled, ugly, orange sheepdog than Charlie.

REAL DOGS

Nicola Laws, Oakey, Queensland

They always baulk at the door, a lifetime of lessons returning to them. People enter buildings, dogs stay out. Strong hands pull at their chains—or the more usual baling twine—dragging them inside.

The vet's surgery is a strange territory of unfamiliar smells and noises. There's an enclosing by roof and walls. Working dogs always think they're in trouble when brought here. Why else would they be made to come inside?

They make up over half of the small animal caseload of the mixed rural veterinary practice at which I work. For me it's possibly the most enjoyable half. We call them Real Dogs—dogs that work for a living. They present us with a spectrum of problems: routine heart worm checks, vaccinations, emergencies like snake bite, baitings or broken limbs. Or those niggling farm dog worries—flea allergy, ear haematoma or mange.

What do they have in common? Looks that won't win them any beauty contests, a rangy body shape, a patch of hair missing here or maybe a broken tooth or crooked ear there. They also have a stoicism rarely seen in other breeds; and an inbuilt trust of humankind, despite only the occasional pat or kind word.

Some are canine Jekyll and Hydes. The same dog we can do anything to at the hospital will eat us for breakfast should we step on their turf. All show a boundless, enduring energy and level of fitness. If a blue or a kelpie can't find trouble, then they're quite likely to go out and make it.

Snow was quite typical of his kind. Then six years old, a kelpie type, pale-eyed and with a coat so sandy it was almost white, he was one of five dogs that enabled his owner to run a cattle property single-handed near Cecil Plains, Queensland.

The district was flood-bound a few years ago, with many properties cut off for up to a week. Snow certainly picked his time to get sick. His owner, a person I had come to respect for his care and concern for all his dogs, rang for advice. There wasn't much to give—start a course of injectible penicillin, keep up the fluids and bring him in as soon as the track was passable.

It was several days before I saw Snow. He was a walking anatomy lesson, so thin that every bone under that staring, dehydrated coat was visible. He had been depressed for days, not eating, and had begun vomiting. The lack of urination suggested kidney failure. The only dry thing at Cecil Plains that week must have been Snow's bladder.

Over the next few days that dog took everything we could dish out to him with good-natured acceptance. Blood tests, intravenous fluids, injections, bladder catheters. The vomiting stopped and he began drinking and urinating litres of fluid. We sent him home, despite the long-term dark cloud over him. Blood results had confirmed severe non-compensating renal failure.

We were never certain of the cause. The farmer had been draining radiators on the property that week, and the rain had resulted in some of the sludge pooling near Snow's kennel. Radiator additives can be very toxic to kidney tissue, and may be quite palatable to dogs. It all seemed to fit together.

I get to see a lot of dogs, and hear a lot of dog stories. Some are real characters or have performed acts of bravery. But there was something about Snow, and dogs like him, which strikes a chord. It's their quiet toughness and ability to survive, with maybe a little help from veterinary science, and that greatest of healing devices— a tincture of time.

Snow comes in every year. He's just a slip of a dog, and still drinks a lot of water. But he can do a day's work when asked. I've always got an extra pat for him when I see him. Because to me, he's a real dog.

THE DOGS OF OLD GLEN HELEN

Bryan Bowman, Alice Springs, Northern Territory

When, in 1938, I took over Glen Helen from Fred Raggatt, he had an old dog called Whiskey and an old bitch called Rosie. Rosie was mothering her last litter of puppies.

Raggatt at first insisted on killing all the pups and leaving the old dog and Rosie with me as he was leaving the Territory for good and going to live in Adelaide. Eventually, however, he agreed to leave three pups.

In three months, the pups—Bully, Snowy and Daisy—were following me through all classes of stock work, though admittedly I sometimes had to carry one of them home in front of me on the horse after a very long day.

Nineteen thirty-eight was a dry year on the north side of the Macdonnell Ranges but in January 1939, there was a big monsoonal rain causing high floods in the Fink, but this didn't dampen the dogs' enthusiasm. We crossed the horses over the Fink in a relatively shallow spot with the water just up to a horse's withers. The dogs not only swam the river but once waterborne, attached themselves to any horse hanging back.

Ten inches fell in one week, followed by a further six inches in February. By April there were plenty of cattle ready for market and we started mustering. We got most of the cattle easily without having to get out of a walk very often.

However, there was a big white cleanskin bull who defied all efforts to put him into the mob. The rest of the mob was complete and ready to move into the trucks with one day to spare, so we decided to make an all-out attack on the white bull. The white bull was well known to the Aboriginal stockmen from Raggatt's time, and usually ran on the slopes of Mt Razorback.

Our plan of action was to hold a mob of quiet cattle on one of the open flats at the foot of Mt Razorback. Two boys were to go round and turn the bull down onto this flat and I was to wait in a strategic position with the dogs.

It worked like a dream. The bull came trotting along with a stock boy to the right and left of him and I joined in with the dogs in the centre.

However, as soon as the bull saw the other cattle and horsemen, he whipped around like a polo pony and headed for his old haunts on Mt Razorback. But at this point the dogs sailed into him. Bully had bull-terrier blood and usually went for the nose. The other two were typical blue heelers and maintained a merciless attack on his heels.

Confusion reigned for some minutes. Bloodcurdling roars of fury came from the bull and an occasional yelp of pain from the dogs. Bully went sailing through the air like a football and I thought it was curtains for him, but he picked himself up and joined the heelers in their ferocious attack on his heels. At this point the bull admitted defeat and ran to the other cattle for protection. Once into the mob he soon quietened down and duly went up the loading ramp in Alice Springs.

Nineteen thirty-nine was a good season and with the assistance of the dogs the whole herd, including the big cleanskins, was branded and the fats disposed of. War had broken out in Europe and a military camp had grown up in Alice Springs bringing restrictions on sending cattle out of the Northern Territory. The good rains of 1939 were not repeated in 1940, which proved to be one of the driest years on record.

By November 1940, cattle were dying along the Fink and it was apparent the whole area had to be destocked within walking distance of the Fink. Most of this area had been completely eaten out. It had been overstocked for years in Raggatt's time, but there had been no alternative to this as he had no other permanent water.

We had opened up two wells on the west side, one on the Dashwood and one on Stokes Creek. It was 45 miles to the nearest well on the Dashwood, a long walk without water for weak cattle.

However, we achieved this feat by waiting for the full moon and travelling through the night. There were minimal losses. We put the cattle together on the Fink about two days before the full moon, gave them a good drink at about five o'clock in the afternoon, had supper and moved off into the copper and gold sunset with the moon now well above the horizon and the dogs bringing up the rear. If at any time a cow or a calf lay down in the scrub, you would hear a commotion and a calf would rush past you back into the mob while the dogs, looking very pleased with themselves, would be eagerly looking for the next one to hang back.

We moved some 2,000 cattle from the Fink area and saved that country around the Fink from being knocked around during that terrible year.

The end of this story is sad and one for which I blame myself to some extent. One very hot day in January 1943 I had to go down to No. 8 Bore to meet Jim Bullen, who was bringing cattle out to stock his Derwent Station. We had killed for rations the night before and the dogs were gorged with blood and offal from the beast. With this in mind I carefully chained the dogs up before leaving, but when I got about two miles down the Dashwood, I saw them following me. They had very small heads and could usually pull their heads out of any collar if they really wanted to. It was getting late and I didn't fancy going back and tying them up again. I decided to let them follow and hope for the best. When I got to the bore there was no water. The dogs were nowhere in sight and I thought they had most likely returned to the station. But in fact, being so full of meat, they had knocked up and must have been lying down somewhere in the scrub.

When I got back to the station and they were not there, I got a fresh horse and a couple of waterbags, and with one of the stock boys went looking for them. But I never saw them again.

I have tried since then to establish a good breed of cattle dog without success.

The day of the cattle dog in the Centre for mustering is over, but they are still used a bit for yard work. This is due to two factors.

First, dogs of today ride too much in Landrovers and utilities and their feet get too soft. A day's work in the Ranges is all they can stand.

Secondly, most of the mustering is done today with helicopters and there is no way dogs can adapt to this kind of work except that one of the disabilities of helicopter mustering is that once cattle get used to the chopper, they are apt to go into thick clumps of scrub and lie down. There is then no way the chopper pilot can shift them.

A couple of good dogs could get them out pronto, but it's hard to see how this could be coordinated with the helicopter. I have never heard of it being tried.

MR BROOKS AND BLUE

Jeff Baldwin, Wangaratta, Victoria

An old man as I remember him, Mr Brooks was the last of the bullockies in our area, the Dandenongs, between 1920 and 1930. Contrary to the popular image of bullockies, he was not loud-mouthed, nor did he swear. Instead he was a kindly, softly spoken man who got things done quietly and efficiently. To my knowledge he had always been a bullock driver.

I daresay he sensed my love for bullocks and dogs, and that's why I was allowed to tag along.

Mr Brooks and Blue, his kelpie cross Queensland heeler, probably had some influence on the choosing of my career. I was allowed to follow along behind the wagon (bare feet in the dust or mud) and turn the wheel that operated the brake! Being allowed to do this probably changed my ambition from being an engine driver like every other young boy at the time, to becoming a bullock driver! (I suppose at 73 years of age I still am a bullocky at heart. In the farm shed hang the bullock yokes an old teamster gave me years ago and I still have the ambition of breaking in my own team.)

When Mr Brooks was yoking his bullocks for the day's work, Blue would heel the bullocks with such ferocity that they would just stand and watch him, too frightened to move away and avoid the yokes being put on.

These days it's hard to visualise an old man yoking up a team of between twelve and twenty bullocks single-handed and without yards, but that's what Mr Brooks did with Blue. The dog would stand by and watch, until asked to take action on any beast that would not get into line.

After the team was yoked and hitched to whatever load they were asked to pull, Blue really came into his own. Bullocks are like humans —they will bludge if given the chance. When this happened, it only needed Mr Brooks to say 'Baldy', 'Ring', 'Brindle', whatever the name was of the offending beast, and Blue would slip in behind the 'bludger', usually unseen, and provide the necessary incentive to correct the bullock's laziness.

In most cases it was not necessary for the dog to heel the guilty bullock because as soon as Mr Brooks spoke its name, it knew what the result would be should it not respond.

I have been working dogs all my life and still am. When I set the gates a certain way, a bitch will muster a 150-acre paddock; when I rub the knife on the steel, a dog will bring in the killers; when bringing up the house cows, the dogs will leave the dry cows behind— and so it goes on. Most farmers have dogs that respond to a given situation.

However, on reflection over the years, Mr Brooks and Blue seem to me to have been the most perfect combination. The dog Blue made it possible for that old man to carry on his profession right up to almost the end of his life. He never had to rely on other people, and more importantly, he did not draw on the public purse for social service, pension or whatever—thanks to Blue, who only ever asked to be fed.

100 MILES BACK TO PATA

Ruth Payne, Victor Harbor, South Australia

We were living on a farm at Pata near Loxton. The boss had a mob of sheep on a property at Pompoota near Murray Bridge, which he checked regularly with the help of his dog Tinker.

One day the boss went to Pompoota and then decided to sell the sheep at the next market. He left his dog with a neighbour until his return.

Back home at Pata, he was up early next morning to do the milking. He missed his usual helper, but out of habit called him anyway, saying, 'Fetch the cows, Tink!'

He was utterly amazed when out from a sheltering bush crept his faithful dog—footsore and weary but ready to work. Tinker had walked 100 miles to get home.

REPAID IN FULL

Mavis Appleyard, Warren, New South Wales

When he was sixteen, my husband Doug found a man ill-treating a young kelpie bitch. After an altercation he took the dog with him and kept her.

He called her Janet and she filled the void in the lonely life he led on a huge sheep station. She quickly became a wonderful, reliable worker, mustering huge paddocks, drafting, penning up, yarding and doing shed work. She knew what to do before she was even told to do it and Doug and she were inseparable.

One day working in the shed at Butterbone Stud Park, Doug was frantically busy and was very annoyed with Janet because she kept disappearing and had to be repeatedly called from under the shearing shed.

By nightfall when he knocked off, Doug was exasperated with her and she finally crept out looking very guilty after much angry calling. In the eight years he had owned her, she had never let him down or left his side when they were working. When she made it obvious she wanted him to check under the shed, he did. In a corner, where the sheep under the shed could not walk on them, were thirteen squealing newborn pups that she had produced between taking mobs in, yarding, penning up and taking sheep away.

Janet repaid us in thousands of ways in her thirteen years for being rescued from a cruel owner by a young boy.

She was a very shy dog and did not like children near her and generally gave them a wide berth. However, after a lot of rain I couldn't find our fifteen month old son. Hearing his annoyed squeals from near the swollen creek, I ran down there and found Janet running between him and the water bumping him sideways away from the water.

She looked very relieved to see me and quickly disappeared and left me to collect him.

LEARNING MY PLACE IN LIFE

Margaret Williams, Yandina, Queensland

Thirty years ago I was governessing for Christopher and Shirley White on Pembroke Station, between Roma and Surat, Queensland. I learned a few valuable lessons while I was there.

One day Ringo, the prized red kelpie sheepdog belonging to Christopher, was knocked down by a car, damaging one of its front legs.

That night, by sheer coincidence, I fell in the bath, hurting my ankle.

Next morning, Chris bundled Ringo and me into his car and drove us 28 miles to the Surat Base Hospital for medical treatment.

The medical superintendent attended to the dog first!

HE FOUND FAME IN THE END

Geoffrey Blight, Narrogin, Western Australia

Gus had been a top trial dog in his day, with wins in four States. He was a short-haired tricolour border collie, South Australian bred and a first generation import of the Scottish Merle that had won the British National title in the seventies. Gus had been runner-up six times to the Dog of the Year in Western Australia, but although he had done well in both field and yard trials, he'd never taken the top award.

He started life as an impossibly headstrong dog, which led to his being sold cheaply in Western Australia, where he enjoyed success under a rigid boss. With age and pressure, he had a few heart problems and was declared past it after failing for a year to show form and even the will to stay on the trial ground. It was decided he should be put down.

A very intelligent dog, he'd attracted the eye of an old contractor, new to dog trials, who had owned only one dog for most of his forty years working on farms. Gus had sired some good pups so after a little pleading and much talk about it being a waste of time, Gus was spared and moved to another home. Everyone involved in dog trials was critical of the newcomer for spending time on a has-been dog who had learnt to quit. 'They don't come back,' was the catchcry.

Old Gus started a new life as a sheep contractor's dog, which entailed handling ewes and lambs daily in portable yards—a very different lifestyle and pressure from handling three wethers in trials.

His new boss nearly gave up when he first tried to force Gus to work. The dog attacked his arm, then returned to the box on the ute. The boss continued on with the job using a couple of rather thick border collies to draft and mules.

Gus sat on the ute for several days, never attempting to work, and it looked as though all the advice had been right. Then one day, the other dogs made a mistake and there was a bad break of lambs they couldn't hold.

No-one noticed old Gus drop down, but when they finally headed the breakaways, they became aware that very few sheep had got out of the yards. Most of the 800 ewes and lambs had been blocked by Gus who was sitting, covering and holding with great skill.

Nothing was said to the dog except a few calls of 'good dog'. As the pen was closed, he hastily returned to the ute, ignoring any encouragement from the workers to return.

It was the first sign that he still had a bit of will to work, so Gus was allowed to just watch without ever being pressed to do anything. It was soon noticed that he had a habit of joining in when things weren't done to his liking.

If the sheep wedged in the entrance, he would drop down, circling, and, with extraordinary skill, go forward to shave off a break and push them scurrying deep into the pen, followed by a well-directed barking push that would pen the resisting ewes and lambs.

He would be seen to circle the incoming flock and collect runaways, weak or blind sheep. Even though ignored, he would bring them in with a skill not often seen, but he still refused any communication with his boss.

One day, his new boss watched with concern as Gus attempted to remove three lambs stuck behind a gate. Their heads were caught in the ringlock fence. Gus, realising they wouldn't back out, gently took each of the week-old lambs by the hind leg and dragged them back around the gate, letting them go to trot off, bleating, to the ewes standing waiting, stamping their defiance at the dog.

The final turnaround came one hot night as the boss sat watching TV. The doors were open to invite a breeze. As he dozed he was awoken by shuffling on the verandah. He looked up to see an old ewe backing through the kitchen into the lounge, followed by old

Gus who was looking at the boss for signs of approval. He'd obviously found the old ewe on the road and decided it should be brought to somebody's attention.

When the boss offered the dog an outstretched hand, this time Gus did not ignore it, or bite it. After helping load the ewe onto the ute, he returned to sit by the boss and the television.

There was an amazing change from then on. The contracting team suddenly had a very skilled look. Gus got dinkum once left to his own resources to fit in and showed some longtime sheep farmers skills they had never seen before. And no-one tried to correct or tell Gus what to do.

The new boss had recently taken up dog trialling, but wasn't doing very well. He had never worked on three sheep. He was used to the pressure of coping with irate farmers in a hurry with plenty of barking, shouting and kicking. Time after time he would be disqualified from a trial for everything from walking backwards to patting the dog. The only time he had completed the course, he had received a score of one, despite his best efforts to imitate the champions, including Gus's former owner.

There was much curiosity among the dog triallers when they saw Gus had been entered again. They'd watched for a year when he failed all over Australia, running away despite being offered everything, including pockets full of meat lumps to try and start him.

The new boss had never even tried to work three sheep with Gus in case the bubble burst. It was a very quiet and subdued bloke who walked out onto the ground with Gus following. Everybody held their breath. The siren went, but Gus pricked his ears and headed for the three wethers.

It wasn't the greatest run, but he tried. That in itself was a miracle as the new boss, rather than command the dog to perform, appeared to follow him around the ground.

Over the next four years, they made the finals of many open trials, not achieving more than an odd place and a fourth in the State Utility Trial, but the pups the new boss bred went on to do it all and Gus became Western Australia's top sire.

Gus became well known in schools and hospitals and was the mainstay in a publicity stunt for the Perth Royal Show when, in a team of six dogs, he drove sheep right through the centre of the city watched by a crowd of 20,000 people, and was featured on all four TV news reports.

Gus worked rabbits, ducks, geese, goats, cows, horses and even roos. He became one of the State's best known sheepdogs, even appearing on BBC television. But Gus had arthritis and it was taking a toll. X-rays showed his joints were welded and he was in pain, despite much treatment. In his fourteenth year, he could no longer work. He had to be lifted into the ute. The time was getting near. He was left at home now, to sit in the drive and organise visitors.

JILL, MATRIARCH
OF CHAMPIONS

Bernard Doyle, Tenterfield, New South Wales

After some experience on sheep and cattle properties, and eight years in the dairy industry, I took up sheepdog trialling in 1957.

At this time I was employed with the Queensland Department of Agriculture and Stock at Winton. About that time we purchased Lava Jill from Mr Jack Forest of Oakleigh, Longreach. Jill was Herdsman bred from Sheba and by Chappie.

We moved from Winton at the end of 1959 and at our first attempt at the Brisbane RNA show in 1960 or 1961, we won the open trial against fairly strong competition. Jill was a determined hard worker and was placed second at the Queensland Championships when aged thirteen years.

She displayed her talents early. My wife Dulcie reared batches of up to 500 laying pullets at the back of our Winton residence. When the small percentage of cockerels in one of these batches was becoming evident (by comb, wing and tail feather development), someone left the gate chain loose.

Soon after, to everyone's surprise, Jill arrived at the back door of our house with all the conspicuous cockerels under control. She had forced the gate and drafted the baby cockerels from the 300 pullets. Jill was eight months of age and had not shown interest in stock at the time.

We are still breeding fairly closely to Jill's bloodline and right now have great grandsons and great grand-daughters working successfully. Kynoona Tess, one of Jill's progeny, now nine years old, has won several open trials and placings from a relatively small number of trials attended.

Tess and I were selected to represent the Queensland Working Sheep Dog Association Inc. at the recent televised *Australian Sheepdog Challenge* conducted at Werribee Mansion near Melbourne. I am a life member of the above Association and am deeply grateful for being selected. The series was broadcast on ABC television as 'A Dog's Life'.

The results of the grand final for those of you who didn't see the program were: First—Doug Connop of Bridgetown, Western Australia with Glenromain Dinny. Second—Sid Cavanagh, Rochester, Victoria with Marlowe Benji. Third—Greg Prince of Dubbo, New South Wales with Rosedale Turbo.

You may be interested in a few points from an article I wrote in 1983 for the *Queensland Agricultural Journal* on the care and training of working dogs.

Select pups from keen, hard-working parents of proven bloodlines. Pups from some bloodlines will exhibit a keen desire to work at first or second sightings of sheep. From others the pups may be eight months or older before they exhibit this desire. It is good to see pups show an early urge to work but excellent dogs have developed from both early and late starters.

Before the command sessions are started the pup must have a name. One syllable names are best since they have a sharp inflection. Throughout a dog's life it will respond best to commands if its name is used occasionally to obtain added attention.

The trainer can assist the pup by watching its facial expression and encouraging it if he sees uncertainty. Should he see stubbornness he may have to scold to the degree necessary.

At the early sessions off the lead allow the pupil a few chances to obey each command. The trainer should stay calm and keep the pup's confidence.

During training 'body talk' is important. It can be an effective aid should the pupil show uncertainty. The trainer can do much to help by using exaggerated body movements.

Most working sheepdogs in Australia originate from strains of 'heading dogs'. Their dominant instinct is to go to the lead of stock and gather them. They should be encouraged to cast out and to keep recasting as more sheep are sighted. It cannot be overemphasised that practice makes perfect. Working dogs are no exception. They keep on improving with practice and guidance.

HOW DID SHE GET THERE?

Doug Harkin, Maryborough, Victoria

I tell this story in an effort to solve a longstanding mystery. Between 25 and 35 years ago, I saw a border collie bitch lying beside the road at the intersection of the Talbot-Wareek and Maryborough-Avoca roads. The latter is now known as the Pyrenees Highway. This intersection is eight miles west of Maryborough and nine miles east of Avoca.

After about two days the dog moved some 300 yards down to our house. It was very noticeable that one hind leg had about six inches cut off it. This looked to have been done by a mower or a binder. The dog's leg appeared to have been professionally repaired so I thought she must be a good dog and made every effort to locate the owner.

After feeding and watering her for a couple of days, during which she was very shy, I showed her a mob of sheep in the yards, but she did not seem interested.

I took them back to the paddock and called her. She very reluctantly followed me. When they were in the middle of the paddock

I said, 'Go way back', and waved my arm. She flew around them with that particular hop and skip owing to one short leg.

She stood up behind them and as I waved my arms she followed every order. From that moment she was my adoring slave and never left my side. If I was in the house, she would lie on the verandah and wait and listen. If I went out the back door she would be there in a flash. Wherever I worked she would curl up nearby but never let me move without her. When she knew which paddocks the sheep were in, and where the gates were, she could practically do all the sheep work herself. While travelling in a vehicle she was alert to danger and would warn the driver with a short whimper. At the house she announced a visitor with a single bark.

If I went away for a few days she would lie under an old sofa on the verandah and only eat enough to keep herself alive. When I came back she was back to her usual self.

My uncle once said, when trying to capture her attention, 'She won't take her eyes off you. She thinks you're bloody marvellous'.

We were inseparable for years and when she died I was very emotionally upset. She was the best and most faithful dog I have ever had in 70 years.

I have often wondered how she was left there—obviously not deliberately. Perhaps a truckie got out to inspect his load, and did not miss her on getting back. Surely, somewhere, there is someone still alive who knew of a marvellous border collie with three legs lost in that area. If so I would love to hear from them.

PART 2

AFTER YEARS
OF WORK TOGETHER

- *The bond that is formed*
- *Trust*
- *Mutual respect*
- *Shared lives*

SANDSOAP

Ron Kerr, Borroloola, Northern Territory

Forty years ago this year I was tailing a mob of bullocks a few miles north of Bourke, New South Wales, along the Darling River at Mays Bend.

The bullocks had come from Nockatunga Station on the Wilson River, south-west Queensland. There were 1,250 head and after droving them for months from Nockatunga, they were well handled and the grass along the Darling was knee-high and green. We were waiting for the Bourke Meatworks, run by Bunny Tankred, to have enough room in the yard to take the bullocks.

It was a drover's dream tailing bullocks on tall green grass alongside clear running river water, compared to the country we had come over, with raw sand, dust, flies and scrub. Already the bullocks were starting to camp only two hours off night camp, about a mile off the river where we would ride night watch.

There were five of us in the camp—a horse-tailer, cook and three of us with the cattle, all taking turns to watch the cattle at night on open, soft ground free from gullies, logs or stumps. The spot for night camp was mostly picked by the cook and horse-tailer—a place where the night watchman had a chance to go with the lead of the cattle if they jumped. And this mob had done plenty of that for the first week out of Nockatunga.

But now they were like milking cows and could be handled by one man. That's why that day I was on my own with the bullocks. It was my turn to tail the cattle.

I left the night camp at daybreak, with my corned beef and damper in the saddlebag and a quart pot on the other side of the saddle as I wouldn't be back to the camp until it was time to bed down the bullocks at dark that evening.

That night I wouldn't have to take a night watch and I was looking forward to a good night's sleep as everyone else in the camp would be sleeping most of that day. It was about dinnertime or midday when the cattle camped along the hollow in the river bed, so I put the quart pot on to boil.

When the horse, tied to the tree, started moving about, snorting now and then, I walked over to check if there were ants about, or whatever else might be upsetting it.

About twenty yards from the horse was a black and tan pup about two months old, and that poor I thought he'd have to stand twice before making a shadow. I felt like getting a good, strong stick and putting him out of his misery. He had big, sad eyes and wasn't frightened to look me in the eye with both of them.

I tried to pat him, but he got up and moved about ten feet away. I tried again. He moved away again. I said, 'OK, you independent bastard. I've got a quart pot boiling away and I've got no use for a dog, as we've never had dogs in the camp.' I went back to making the tea.

Getting my corned beef and damper out of my saddlebag, I'd just sat down when I heard something behind me. Looking around, there was the pup with his big, sad eyes sitting under the shade near the horse. I thought, 'I'll win this dog over to my way of thinking.'

Breaking off some corned beef, I walked over to him, getting on the upwind side so he could smell the beef. It was no go. He could smell the meat all right. I could see his nose twitching, but he wouldn't come to me or let me touch him. It was just those big, goggle eyes that said nothing.

I threw the meat towards him. It hit the ground about six inches in front of his nose. I think it was still moving when it disappeared and I saw the lump snaking down the pup's throat. There was not even a wag of the tail. Just those big glassy eyes looking at me, or at something above my head.

I had finished eating as much corned beef as I wanted and still had plenty left over. From habit I always carry more corned beef than I need in case there is trouble with the cattle. You may miss a mealtime and beef was not short in this camp; and the more you ate, the better you were paid.

So, going to my horse to check out the cattle, I emptied what left-over food I had not far from the dog—who never made a move towards the meat. Riding away, I looked back. The pup was eating, so I left him to it and rode around the bullocks.

Half an hour later I was sitting on my horse under some shade overlooking the bullocks camped along the grassy hollow when the horse tried to get a look behind him. I turned around and there was

Big Eyes sitting under a tree twenty yards away. This went on every time I moved. The pup moved like he was some sort of tail-light.

About 3 o'clock the bullocks were on their feet starting to feed. I was kept busy working the bullocks out of the river, making them feed out over the river flats towards the camp. It was near sundown when I looked to see if the pup had followed. Sure enough, there he was, even though his eyes looked the biggest part of him.

Just on dark the horse-tailer came out and gave me a hand to put the cattle on camp as he could then take my horse out to the others and hobble him, and bring back another night horse. With the cattle bedded down, I picked up my swag and took it over near where the night horses were tied up. Although I wasn't watching that night, I had to be up and on a horse if the cattle jumped.

The horse-tailer came up with the last night horse and asked where the bony, big-eyed pup came from. I told him he'd been following me at a distance all day along the river and I didn't want to chase him away as he might run into the bullocks and spook them. And as he was over near my swag I'd try to catch him and tie him up that night in case he put the cattle on their wheels.

The horse-tailer said, 'If you can fatten him you might see that he has a bit of breeding in him.' I said the breeding might be a long way in and the way he eats beef we might need the whole mob to fatten him. But the horse-tailer said, 'He's a black and tan kelpie and could be close to purebred and they don't bark much unless they're made to bark.'

That night when I went to my swag with a piece of fresh cooked corned beef, I was going to try to catch Big Eyes and tie him up with one of my swag straps. I started feeding him little bits of meat at a time. Each piece was gulped down but I still couldn't get a hand on him. At last I gave him all the meat. The way his gut came out you could see where the beef was.

A few days later, we moved off with the bullocks to the meat-works yards. There our long trip from Nockatunga finished and Big Eyes was there twenty yards behind me all the time.

From there, I looked up my brother, Frank, who was camped with his droving plant at North Bourke. Me and Big Eyes camped with Frank for a week or so, then a mate of mine came along looking for someone to go with him up on the Culgoa River towards the Queensland border mustering sheep for shearing.

So next day, me and Big Eyes left for Kennibree Station walking a plant of horses. Big Eyes wouldn't get up under the wagonette with the other dogs, so he followed me behind the horses for the 40 miles. By now, he was in my shadow all the time and I could put my hand on him. But he never wagged his tail. He just lay down and looked at me like I was stupid.

My mate Wally Smith said, 'He's a one-man dog if ever I saw one and if you just give him time, he'll make a worker and a good one at that. But you want to call him a name, and one that someone can't pick if you lose him. Big Eyes is too close to his looks.'

A few days later, we were washing our clothes down at the creek and Wally said, 'Have you worked out a name for the dog yet?'

I said I'd tried every dog's name I know and there was still no reaction. As I had a cake of sandsoap in my hand for washing, I said I might as well call him Sandsoap. The dog stood up and wagged his tail for the first time. Smithy said, 'That's close to his name. Call him Sandy.'

The reaction was now from the ears and tail.

Smithy said, 'Make it Sandsoap. It's harder for someone else to think of.'

So, Sandsoap it was. I now had a dog with a name and one I could pat, tie up and which had meat over his ribs.

For the next two days of mustering sheep, Sandsoap never got any more than ten feet from my horse, but he jumped up and down when Wally's dog went around the sheep.

Wally rode around the mob saying to me, 'Has Sandsoap taken any interest yet?'

I said, 'He goes ten feet from the horse and I go the rest. And he's supposed to be a sheepdog.'

Next morning, we were taking shorn sheep back to a paddock. I said to Wally, 'I'll tie this Soap ad up as he might cause trouble.'

Wally said, 'No. Bring him along. These shorn sheep're hungry and they'll take some holding until we get out onto some grass country.'

There was a small holding paddock near the shearing shed with about 1,000 shorn sheep, all snow white. Wally said for me to go down and open the gate and try to steady the lead of the sheep when they went through.

I opened the gate and out came the sheep. Now to steady the lead.

There was no lead. They were all round the horse, under the horse's belly and I was trying to get the horse to the outside. Finally reaching the outside, I looked for Sandsoap. Was he still in the middle under the sheep? I noticed that Wally's dogs must have blocked the lead as the dogs were starting to turn them back.

Getting to the lead, I saw Sandsoap doing about 30 miles an hour right across and just under the noses of the sheep. To give him moral support, I yelled, 'Stick it into 'em, Sandsoap.'

That sent him mad. He went around the lead and down the other wing. About 40 yards down the wing, he turned and came back, bringing the other point of the wing around and across the lead. I got out of his way as the lead came bolting around the rest of the mob. I sat there on my horse and couldn't see a thing. There was a red cloud of dust 50 feet in the air.

Wally came around the other side of the mob covered in red dust, saying, 'That dog's starting to work.'

I said, 'He's gone mad and deaf. I can't call him back.'

Wally said, 'Don't try. He's ringing them back onto the fence and will stop ringing soon.' Sure enough, the dust was lifting as the sheep pulled up. Out of the dust came Sandsoap, his tongue almost on the ground and the goggle eyes were like fire. Watching the sheep, he almost ran into us before he saw us.

Wally said, 'I'll bet anything he's a born lead dog, a dog that wants to work on his own. Catch him, and hold him until I bring the tail up. Let the lead go for a while, then we'll give him the lead to work.'

By now, we were coming into grass country and the sheep were settling down, but still moving and spreading. I let Sandsoap go. His tongue was still hanging out, but he trotted across the tail of the mob, stopped once, looked back, then loped off up the wing. Later we could see him trotting back and forth across the lead.

The shed cut out three weeks later and I stopped on the station as overseer for the next three years. Sandsoap started as a jackeroo pup and went on to be head stock dog.

I saved some money, bought a truck and went back droving.

Sandsoap was well known around the drovers' camps and I had a mob of cattle to bring from Quilpie in Queensland to Bourke, about seven to eight weeks' walk.

My brother Frank had 5,500 sheep heading down the Darling to Wentworth. He needed a lead dog, and as I didn't need Sandsoap with cattle, he went to the Vic border on a job he liked best.

We both arrived back at Bourke about the same time, where Frank gave me news about Sandsoap. Having finished the job to

Wentworth, and coming home back up the road along the Darling, Sandsoap fell off the back of the truck and hanged himself.

Frank said he was in a hurry to catch the punt over the river at Louth before the operator headed for the pub at Louth, where it would be hard to make anyone hear you after dark. One of his men had got out of the truck to check the load and found Sandsoap hanging. He unhooked him and put him off the road.

I didn't miss the dog much until I had nearly 8,000 sheep going down the Darling and across to Swan Hill on the Vic border, some three months after Sandsoap was hanged. I crossed over the punt at Louth and was going down the west side of the Darling.

I was at Dunlop Station with 8,000 sheep, very little feed and a mob of sore-footed dogs, when a fellow from Dunlop Station came down the road on horseback and with a dog. As he came level with the lead of the sheep about half a mile from the tail, I saw a dog branch off and go across the lead of the sheep. The bloke I had up on the other wing near the lead started coming back and the bloke that was to pilot us through came on down to the tail where I was. We both arrived on the tail of the mob about the same time. The station man said he'd left his dog up the lead as it was the only place he'd work. My man said he was a good lead dog, too.

Me and this station bloke rode along behind the sheep, him telling me about his dog in the lead, and me telling him about my dog Sandsoap, and how they worked very much the same. You didn't see much of them, but you knew they were up there as the lead was being kept square across the face and every now and then the lead would be bumped back. Everything Sandsoap could do, this bloke's dog, Bandy, could do, and I was beginning to think that this bloke was a parrot. I thought there wasn't another dog in the country that could work as well as Sandsoap. Everyone that knew him reckoned he was the best dog they'd seen.

We were pulling into dinner camp and I said to this bloke, 'Pull your dog in, mate, and give him a blow and a drink.'

He said, 'He'll come in when the sheep start to camp.'

I felt like hanging one on him because Sandsoap wouldn't leave the sheep until the sheep had started to camp. Then I thought, 'How did this bloke know that? I never told him.' And I said, 'Do you want to sell him? I could use a good lead dog and you could buy a good dog for five pounds.' So I offered him ten quid. He said he was not for sale.

Just then, the dog came from behind. I couldn't believe my eyes. The dog was the same colour black and tan, had the same goggle eyes. The bloke called the dog Bandy and it was heading for him. I was at the fire twenty yards off the line the dog was taking when the bloke called out, 'Bandy'. I called, 'Sandsoap'. The dog stopped and came straight for me, jumping all over me.

The bloke from the station said, 'You must have a way with dogs. That's the first time I've seen him go near anyone else.'

I said, 'We've been talking about the same dog all morning.'

He said, 'It can't be. You said your brother had him when he was hung.'

'That's right,' I said. 'But it was only 25 miles back along the road to Louth where he was supposed to have been hanged. He must've been unconscious when they left him. How long have you had this dog?' I asked him.

He said, 'I came five months ago and I was here about a month when the dog turned up. He was very sick and couldn't eat much.'

He asked how long it had been since my brother was through here. I told him it had been three months and three weeks.

'Are you sure he's your dog?' he asked. 'Prove he's your dog.'

I said, 'You send him around the sheep and I'll stop him within ten feet without calling his name.'

He sent him. The dog just started to gallop and I gave a sharp whistle. The dog went down to ground. I said for him to send him again. This time I let the dog get further away and I stopped him again. Then I said, 'I'll send him. You stop him by name.'

I sent him and he called him, 'Bandy', then again, 'Bandy'. I let the dog go until he was at the sheep, then whistled. Down went the dog.

The bloke got up and said, 'He's yours, all right.'

I said, 'Yes, a bloody ghost dog.'

The station bloke left the camp minus Sandsoap, but with twenty pounds in his pocket. After that, Sandsoap was known as the ghost dog around the drovers' camps.

He was run over by a truck out of Broken Hill in 1958. That time he didn't return.

CHANCE

Robert Ellis, Duckmaloi via Oberon, New South Wales

In 1941 my father went to war. He was in the 8th Division which was devastated during the fall of Singapore, where he died.

He had a two-tone tan kelpie dog named Chance, who besides being a good sheepdog was also his very good mate. We lived during this time on Round Hill, a property at Eugowra owned by my uncle. Round Hill was three miles from Eugowra on the Cowra railway line.

Each day a motor train came from Cowra to Eugowra, arriving at 9.30 am and departing at 4 pm for the return journey. On leaving for the war, Dad's first trip was on this motor train, leaving from a point at Round Hill where his family and dog saw him off. I was at this stage not yet one year of age.

We lived for a further two years at Round Hill, where each day Chance went down to the spot where my father boarded the motor train. He always left, rain, hail or shine, just on 4 pm and arrived just before the train went past. He stayed there for a further ten or fifteen minutes before returning home.

He wouldn't work for my uncle or anyone else after Dad had gone.

Two years later we shifted into town, where, again when loose, he left our house about 3.30 pm and trotted along the railway track until he came to the site where he always lay down waiting for the train to go past.

After it had passed he waited about ten minutes, looking down the track, and then slowly trotted off home again.

This went on for a further three years until one day, old and sick, he didn't return.

He was found dead, where he last saw my dad.

I still have descendants of Chance today. They display the same devotion.

HAPPY FATHER'S DAY

Geoffrey Blight, Narrogin, Western Australia

It's a few years ago now, just two days before Father's Day. The phone rang, summoning me to Busselton Hospital, 200 kilometres away. My father had just been admitted, unconscious after collapsing at his home.

A third generation sheepman, Dad had retired three years earlier after being struck down with a heart attack on the family farm. After a short hospital stay Dad had hung up his boots and took Mum, who was also in poor health, and they went paddling together in the sea, to live out their remaining life.

For Dad, that break away was not like him at all as the farm had been his beginning and, simply, his life—a life totally dedicated to the simple devotion to his family of three, and twelve grandchildren.

Also a life of love and dependence on the land, the sheep, the dogs and the horses that he had shared his 67 years with. All these he left behind after that first hospital stay.

What we didn't know, because he told no-one, was that he had cancer and he felt he owed it to Mum, something she had desired, something she had earned over 44 years—a rest and some friends to talk and share a break with from the never-ending battle of the problems the man on the land faces.

And so they went, not looking back as they said goodbye, everyone not really understanding but still happy for them, all bar Rusty—and Rusty missed Dad.

For Rusty was an ageing farm dog, a big, red, long-haired mongrel kelpie who had worked with Dad every single day for about nine years. Dad was a hard master—the dog went on the chain at night, he was not allowed inside and he did as he was told. But Dad loved him and he shared those working days with him, morning to night. Every hour of light they were together. Fencing, driving sheep, whatever it was, there they were, the old ute, Dad and his dog.

There was nothing for a dog like Rusty where Dad was going, only the chain, and that wasn't the way a man likes to see his best friend end, so they had to say goodbye.

Rusty worked those three years, a bit here, a bit there, but it wasn't the same. So often I would find him sitting on the disused old ute, just looking, just waiting, just hoping.

At the hospital they told me that they had already done investigative surgery. Dad had massive abdominal cancer, his bowels were blocked. He had been fitted with artificial pipes and bags, but his chances of more than a few days were very remote. Mum wanted me to tell him rather than the doctor. She felt I might be more of a comfort to him.

Because of the drugs and the operation Dad was too dazed to talk to that day. I had shared the ride with my sister to the hospital so I was obliged to borrow my father's car to return to the farm, and then drive back again on Father's Day, to see him through to the end.

The car sat in the yard next day and an old dog strutted around and around it, ever watchful, looking and waiting, fighting any canine that was game to draw too near. The scent was strong, his hopes were up but the hand or the voice never came.

I lay awake all night and pondered on how and what to say to my father. 'Thank you, Dad. I love you, Pop. Goodbye. God bless and Happy Father's Day,' but nothing came and with dawn I just felt confusion and sadness as we prepared to leave.

A phone call from Mum told me that Dad was being allowed home for an hour to share Father's Day with his entire family, who by now had begun gathering, and still the words wouldn't come. 'Remember the old days, Dad. Don't worry, Dad. We won't forget you, Dad.' They just weren't right.

Dressed and ready to go as dawn broke I stood by the car door, looking down on the ageing dog while waiting for all the family to get themselves settled in the car. The sad, disappointed eyes still searching, looking, hoping, pleading.

I opened the door and for what reason I still don't know, I told the old dog to get in. The ears came up, the scent was stronger, it had been a long time since he had sat in there. Maybe, just maybe.

All hell broke loose when my well-dressed family now had to share space with the hairy old dog.

'Why in the name of fortune does he have to go? There's no room. Don't be stupid. Get that dog out of the car.'

The spur of the moment idea didn't enjoy any support and matters didn't improve when we reached Busselton.

'What are you going to do with the dog? There's nowhere to put him. He'll start a fight with Rex. Get him out of here.' And so, after three hours of hoping, Rusty was bundled into the garden shed, out of the way before we went to get Dad for that precious hour.

He looked very sick, very tired. He coughed blood every few minutes as he tried to smile and to be happy but he knew, he had known all along, that this day would come. At least he had made Mum happy these last three years and they had been happy, the walks, the swims, the grandchildren, the peace, time to remember.

We put Dad on a bed in the loungeroom, propped up with pillows. Grandchildren everywhere, muted chatter—'How are you? ... Anything I can get you? ... Hello, Poppa.'

Everyone wanted to speak but no-one could think of what to say. All were uneasy. I went for a walk on the beach. I could take it no longer.

Later they told me they were going to have some photos taken of the grandchildren with Pop when the barking started. Pop, needing something to say, asked to see Rex, Mum's pet labrador, which was making most of the noise. Mum let Rex inside. He sent things flying as he bounded around everyone, forcing them out of his way and so had to be banned outside to the shed, with a departing smile and a pat from Dad.

No-one had mentioned Rusty and Mum didn't know what to do as Rusty had never been in a house in his life. Dad never spoke of him but here, eyes shining at her, his old ears up, Rusty was pleading to be let out.

Twenty people stood in the loungeroom, the camera ready. They were about to take a picture we could all remember, one last shot of Pop and the family he loved. Everyone was restrained. They kept looking away, the words just wouldn't come.

Then another entered the room. He came quietly and fast, his head held high, the eyes glistening, ears up, now the scent was stronger. Between the legs he came. All stared but no-one said a word. The old dog only looked ahead, tail wagging, and then their eyes met.

Only the old dog moved, a slight bound and four hairy paws rested on the bed. Glistening eyes stared at each other in a silent room. As the long nose reached out, the soft moist tongue touched a hardened old cheek, the tears, shining and silent, joined together and rolled uncontrolled down a very sick but happy face.

It was then I met all the family walking quietly along the beach.

They had left what was left of the hour to Mum, Dad and Rusty.

When we did return to the house it was time for me to take Dad back. Nobody touched or spoke to Rusty. He just sat by the bed and as we moved Dad into a wheelchair, out he followed.

Everyone was saying goodbye or volunteering to go back with him to the hospital, but Dad just smiled and thanked them and beckoned Rusty into the back of the car, asking that only he accompany us.

I could not say anything as we drove the four miles back. I just stole a glance occasionally at the strained faces looking forward, the old dog now standing on the back seat, his nose only inches from the old man's cheek.

Nothing whatsoever was said between man and dog. At the hospital entrance I lifted Dad into the wheelchair. He stared straight ahead. No words, not even a glance at Rusty. As I moved the chair back to shut the car door, the old dog sat, nose pressed hard against the glass. Still the old man stared ahead, now visibly upset and trembling.

For a moment I thought I might say something but could not. As I started to push the chair away an old hand suddenly came out and bony old fingers pressed hard against the glass. Their eyes met for the last time and in a moment not meant for me, the old man, tears streaming freely down his cheeks, mumbled, 'Goodbye, old boy,' and we slowly moved away.

They are both dead now. Dad was carried to his final resting place by his tearful young grandsons, his witness read solemnly and sincerely by loving grand-daughters. The man who believed 'Family is Forever' presented his credentials to his maker.

But on the last page of a family album that spans 44 years of a happy and very successful marriage is a picture of an old man, tears rolling down his cheeks, his hands outstretched to his workmate, his friend, taken in the loungeroom on that final Father's Day. A loving family left all the words to a hairy old dog to deliver and by the photo rests a card which reads:

Dad

A gift for today I have not bought
On this Father's Day our time is too short.
Forgive me then for hoping this way

To take you back to yesterday
When times were hard and times were good
The times we'd relive, if only we could.
The cold morning air, the midday sun
When twilight came our work was done.
So I've brought your mate who lived them too
Who like all of us, shares a love for you.

PINING FOR THE PAST

Mrs Mac, Lake Cathie, New South Wales

We had a small farm on the outskirts of Grafton. Our dog was a blue heeler named Rover.

When we got rid of the few cattle we had, Rover used to walk our big black rooster around the paddock all day long, every day.

One sad day my grandfather died. We then discovered that the dog was always missing between 10 am and 11.30 am every day. We used to wonder where he went.

The grave-digger who lived not far from us told us that if we were looking for Rover between these times, we would always find him lying on his master's grave.

I took a photo of him on my grandfather's grave and keep it in my collection.

FOR NO-ONE BUT DAD

Carolyn McConnel, Esk, Queensland

I was leaving Brisbane, where I had been working, to get married, and I wanted to give Dad something special in thanks for all he had done for me. In the *Queensland Country Life*, some kelpie pups in New South Wales were advertised for sale, but the ad said they could be railed anywhere in Queensland. I wrote asking for a black and tan bitch pup.

The office at the Roma Street Railway Station seemed deserted when I went to collect the pup, but finally a porter arrived to say he had found it, but as it had looked hungry, they had taken her down to the canteen and given her a feed.

To my horror, a large black belly with a head and four feet was handed over to me. It appeared she had eaten very well indeed and was in some danger of bursting.

By the time we had driven out to my parents' property at Ilfracombe in western Queensland, some 800 miles away, she was looking more like a pup and less like a balloon. Dad was very pleased to get her as his old dog was slowing up and it was time to start training a replacement.

He called her Coco as she really was a very elegant-looking dog. She quickly took to work and to riding around on the back of Dad's motorbike, and she was very much his dog. She tolerated the rest of the family, but took orders from no-one but Dad.

The one thing that really stood out was her uncanny ability to know from what direction Dad was returning when he was away in the property's Cessna. A lot of other planes flew over every day, but she took no notice of them. When Dad flew off, she would go and camp in the shade somewhere.

Some time later you would see her get up and go out onto the area near Dad's office and she would sit peering into the distance. You would then know that Dad was on his way home. We would not hear the plane for a good ten minutes, but Coco always knew and she always sat facing the way he was approaching. Sometimes we'd laugh at her, knowing that Dad had gone west and there she'd be, facing east. But sure enough, something would have happened and he'd have had to go somewhere else and would be coming back from the east.

Even when he went to Brisbane for a few days, the day he was due home, about a quarter of an hour before he arrived, old Coco would be sitting outside the office watching for him.

Once he had landed she would wander down to the hangar to help put the plane away and just check he was back safely. Then she would camp outside the garden fence, keeping an eye out in case he needed her help with anything.

She really was a wonderful old dog, as loyal as any dog to her owner and she was sadly missed when she finally died of old age.

A LONG WEARY WAIT

Joy Combe, Crystal Brook, South Australia

My father got a young kelpie pup from a neighbour and we named it Brown Towser.

Before Jim and I were married, we used to go for long walks in the hills and Brown Towser pup liked to come with us. After a little while, she would usually get tired and Jim would pick her up and carry her. As a result, whenever she got tired, she would jump up into Jim's arms to be carried.

Jim went away with the RAAF during the 1939 to 1945 war. After several years, he came home on leave.

My father and Towser were bringing sheep up from the front paddocks past the house to the hills at the back. When Towser saw Jim, she left my father and the sheep, and dashed across to Jim. She immediately jumped up into his arms and stayed a few minutes before racing back to my father and the sheep again.

NOT ON SPEAKING TERMS

Denis Adams, Apsley, Victoria

When I went to Jabuk in 1952, one of our neighbours was Alan Ross, a man ahead of his time in the control of sand drift. He was one of the nicest blokes you'd ever meet, but even old Alan could be temporarily unpopular.

One day I found him hard at work in the sheep yards. And 'hard' was the operative word! Normally his large, plump sheepdog bitch Trixie did just about everything except work the drafting gate. This day, however, Trixie was not her usual, busy self. She was acting like a wife whose husband had forgotten her birthday.

She would half fill the yard, then pause to give Alan a dirty look.

'Come on, Trixie,' he would urge. Then, with a look that plainly said 'Humph', she would disdainfully run a few more in.

'What's up with Trixie?' I asked.

'Oh, she's not speaking to me today,' Alan told me, looking embarrassed. 'You know how humid and stinking hot it was yesterday, before we had that bit of a thunderstorm? Well, I was feeling so tired and crook with this damn boil on my backside, I thought I'd take a spell. I was lying on my belly out on the bed on the verandah.'

Coming from Alan, this was an amazing admission. Normally he ran rings around all us young blokes. He was a workaholic!

'Trixie was asleep under the bed,' he went on. 'Then all of a sudden there was a terrific clap of thunder. She got such a scare that she jumped up on top of me—fair on my boil!'

Alan, it seemed, had risen vertically some distance above the bed. With a howl of agony, he had lashed out instinctively at poor, terrified Trixie.

'I didn't mean to kick the old girl,' he told me sadly. 'I was sorry as soon as I'd done it, but she still hasn't forgiven me!'

NOT THE BEST DOG
IN HIGHBURY

Geoffrey Blight, Narrogin, Western Australia

Standing on the side of the road on a cool April afternoon never struck me as being the place I might hear a great dog story. So when a familiar ute pulled up as I herded a mob of crutched weaners into the paddock, I hardly could have guessed the outcome.

It was old Bill. I'd known him all my life. He was of my father's generation and Dad's mate. Dad's been gone ten years and I'm a grandfather, so old Bill is no longer young.

Bill never married. A very shy chap. I'd had many talks with him over the years.

'I've been reading your yarns,' he said.

I sensed there was something more. Bill wasn't the reading type, but as we talked he again came back to the dog story of mine he'd read.

'If I tell you a dog story, you won't laugh, will you?'

He didn't have to ask.

'I haven't told anyone in fifty years, but you might be able to tell me why it happened.'

Bill's old face, wrinkled with age, almost blushed and I wondered at his shyness.

Bill was the last of a family that had pioneered Highbury. We had buried his brother a fortnight before.

'Your uncle gave me a dog once,' he began. 'A black kelpie called Jack. Not the best sheepdog in Highbury, but he did me and we got on all right.'

The story I now repeat was told uninterrupted on the side of a gravel track that fifty years before had seen Bill, his old dad and Jack travel four miles to the Highbury siding at midnight. There Bill caught the train and went to war.

His kelpie Jack was his only possession and his dad promised to look after the wayward old bastard. He told Bill to take care and to come home as soon as he could. Bill stood at the train window and stared at the old ute's fading lights. He was filled with restlessness and fear as he left his father and dog in that dark railway yard.

Bill had mates going also. Soon the homesickness gave way to a sense of adventure. The whole world was before them, but not for long. War makes young men grow up fast and Bill was no different. He soon learnt about the fear and tragedy of the cost of lives. Unlike the others, he didn't have a girl back home, making him feel left out when the blokes spoke of getting back to their women. He used to think of old Jack and wonder how he was going.

His mother sent letters. There weren't many and they were not very well written. They told him Jack was still Jack, still no better at rounding up sheep. Things seemed to be always grim. It was who had fallen or been injured, or how terrible the grain and wool prices were. But—they were from home.

Bill lost a close mate. Everybody did. There was no-one to tell. He wondered why he was there. He was sent to Queensland for retraining for the jungle. The Allied position was bad. The Japanese were advancing through New Guinea and already bombing Darwin. It looked like a certain attack on Australia.

Bill had not had home leave for years. Suddenly, he was told to go home and see his folk before being sent to the Islands. Not permitted to tell anybody, nor allowed to write or phone, he was issued rail passes for travel. The Defence Force didn't want troop movements known or recorded anywhere. It took Bill eleven days to get on the 'Midnight Horror' that would take him home to Highbury. Everybody was frightened and depressed. The war was going badly.

Even though he had been travelling for eleven days, it seemed an eternity to wait at Narrogin station. The people had a midnight cuppa and the slow Albany train passed through, on its way to Perth. The trains always passed each other at Narrogin, so the first there had to wait.

Finally they were rolling again. Bill stood in the rocking gangway looking out into the gloom, knowing that only a mile further was home—and Jack. It had been too long. No light showed in the darkness.

Suddenly Bill felt good. He was nearly home. He realised that he would have to walk back four miles, but what the hell. There weren't any guns here. Not yet anyway. How great it would be to see his parents and Jack. God, I hope he's still alive, thought Bill. He would be old now for a dog.

There were no lights in Highbury. No-one to meet the train. The train slowed and finally halted as the guard, with a lantern, jumped down to drop a solitary parcel. Bill jumped down into the darkness. There was no platform. The train immediately shuddered and began its slow choo, choo, choo before slipping away into the night. Suddenly Bill lived a magic moment of his life. He has never forgotten. It led him down the road to tell me fifty years later. About the dog who wasn't the best sheepdog in Highbury. The dog that jumped up to greet him in the pitch darkness that night and embrace him.

Bill was never an emotional man. Very much the opposite. Never one to have admitted a tear, but on this occasion, even as he told me fifty years later, his eyes glistened as he remembered.

'You know, I'm glad no-one was watching. I couldn't help it. I broke down and cried. You know that bloody dog was worth fighting for.'

Although he asked discreetly later, nobody had ever seen Jack in Highbury. No-one knew whether he was there when the midnight trains came in. It was four miles to where he lived.

'How was it,' asked Bill, 'did he know I was coming home?'

'Another funny thing,' Bill went on, 'after I walked home with Jack, I didn't wake the parents. I just went off to my room and went to bed. At daylight, Dad came in carrying a cup of tea.'

'I knew you were home the minute I saw old Jack this morning,' was his quiet way of saying 'welcome home, son'.

Bill said, 'He would never tell me why he made the cup of tea before checking, or whether he had ever brought over a cuppa when I wasn't home.'

Those were secrets Bill's father died with.

'That's why I never told anyone about Jack,' Bill said. 'I don't think they would have believed me.'

44

WEDDED BLISS

Marj Wood, Benalla, Victoria

Skipper was married to the boss long before I was. He wasn't very thrilled with my arrival and made sure I knew that the boss was *his*. In Skipper's opinion the management order was the boss, Skipper and 'her', a very poor third.

Early in our marriage I used to love riding in the back of the ute, with the cold wind blowing in my face as we roared along the narrow dirt roads. Skipper refused to ride in the back with 'her', choosing instead to sit on the passenger seat next to the boss.

When the stock crate was on the back of the ute, I'd squeeze through the gate and into the back, while Skipper sat disdainfully in the front with the boss.

Seeing the ute go past with the boss's wife inside the stock crate and his dog up front beside him, the locals decided that here was one farmer who had his priorities right.

TEAM EFFORT

Marina Hanstock, Parkes, New South Wales

My grandfather had two sheepdogs, Blue and Trixie. In May of 1942, Grandfather was lopping kurrajong to feed to the cattle. He fell from the tree and was badly injured.

Blue walked home, about three miles, while Trixie stayed with my grandfather and kept the cattle at bay. Every time my grandmother came outside, Blue would bark and run in the direction he had come from. After a while Gran followed Blue back to where my grandfather was lying. Gran had to walk a mile for help.

Three days later my grandfather died.

'NO DOGS!'

Kath Frost, Port Macquarie, New South Wales

An unprecedented wet occurred in far western Queensland a few years ago.

Because of the vastness and the low nature of the land, the heavy rains were very worrying for the landholders. To save their stock, great herds of cattle had to be moved miles to high ground. The task would have been impossible to handle without the valued and untiring assistance of the blue heelers that worked with the stockmen.

After days of hard driving, they finally got their cattle to the only high land for miles, and it was then that they found that they, too, were stranded. There was nothing they could do but free their horses, and settle down with their saddles and dogs to wait.

Fortunately, after a couple of days a helicopter flew to their rescue. The pilot got out of his craft and surveyed the dirty, tired and hungry stockmen with their mud-covered dogs. He yelled to them, 'G'day, fellers. Get aboard, but *no dogs!*'

The hungry and weary men, astounded at the thought of leaving their dogs behind, yelled back over the noise of the chopper blades, 'We don't go without our dogs,' and no threats or cajoling could make them change their minds. The pilot was, in the end, forced to concede to their demands.

These highly trained blue heelers were a very valuable asset to the stockmen, as well as being much loved. How could they have left them behind?

SCARLET THE PROTECTOR

Kerry-Anne Bourke, Tallawang, via Gulgong, New South Wales

When Scarlet was about sixteen weeks old and was being broken in, I was drafting some sheep. A neighbour's wethers, western-bred and 'crazy', had got through my fence. A few of these sheep ran into me and knocked me down in the yard. As quick as a flash, this miniscule pup pounced onto me, barred her teeth and barked like something possessed to keep the sheep from trampling me.

To this day, if I go into the yards, she walks between my legs barking and will not let the sheep come near me. I have told many people about this but wasn't believed until recently.

I was working at a friend's shed, and her husband was working next to me, penning up. Suddenly Scarlet jumped into the yard and began frantically barking from between his legs. We were both in jeans and she must have thought his legs were mine.

A LAST FAREWELL

Nyree Renney, Berriwillock, Victoria

As we headed off to Nandaly, we knew we had a sad day ahead of us. Pat Conlan, the father of a very close friend of ours, had died suddenly on the Sunday night from a heart attack at the age of fifty-three.

Arriving at the funeral, we weren't surprised to see five to six hundred people. Pat had been a pillar of the local community, a leading farmer in the district, a wonderful husband and father to six strapping sons.

However, we were surprised to see a sheepdog tied to the church gate. He was greeted by a few as they went through to the small country church and we decided he must have been Pat's working dog.

A few hundred people were standing outside the church and as the service conducted by Father Coffey went along, we all became more and more aware of the dog. Each time the congregation was asked to pray, the dog would howl. After a reading or eulogy was finished, he would howl again.

To this day, I feel a wonderment at the dog's action—although, after all, he had probably spent as much time with Pat as anyone. One certainly got the feeling that Patrick Conlan and his dog had been soul mates.

The dog continued on with the family to the cemetery and once again acted as though he were grieving for his master.

At the luncheon after the funeral, the dog arrived again and was put in the kindergarten playground. He was a little lighter hearted there.

Everyone who attended the funeral commented at some time on this dog and his actions. They also commented on what a moving and loving tribute to her husband it was for Marie to remember the dog at such a tragic time and give him an opportunity to say a last farewell to his master and very obviously best mate. It was the most moving funeral I've ever been to. The dog's name was Oscar.

COMPLETE TRUST

Mavis Ingram, Bega, New South Wales

This is a story about a very old working border collie dog called Socks.

Socks had a very sore front paw and had been carrying it for about a week. Paul and I had tried a few times to find the problem but as Socks didn't like people around him with a needle and scissors, we tended to let him go.

But another week passed and it was no better, so Paul held Socks's mouth while I had a real poke around with the needle. After about ten minutes of trying, I let his paw go and said, 'Socks, I just can't find it to get it out.'

Socks gave a whimper, looked at me and put his paw back in my hand.

I knew I had his trust, so Paul didn't hold his mouth. I did some pretty hard and cruel squeezing and prying with the needle and at last a grass seed and heaps of pus came out from between his toes.

As I gave him a cuddle and pat he gave me a small growl as if to say, 'Thank you.'

That is the closest I have ever felt to an animal. I had his complete trust.

GOOD MATES ARE HARD TO FIND

Mark Thompson, Mapleton, Queensland

I remember the first time we met on the track
I was feeling down with me lot
And you wandered up to me fire
And tipped over me old quart pot.

Aw, I thought to meself—what an idiot
This mongrel will never do.
Then you took off the lid to me camp oven
And stuck your face in me stew.

You ate all of me freshly made damper
And gave out with a cough and a fart,
Had a scratch and a yawn, then you silly red prawn,
You leaked on the end of me tarp.

But there were some things you did quite naturally
That earned my respect and my trust.
Like that time we were out west and droving
That night when the cattle rushed.

I remember how me horse stumbled
You know, the new one, the grey.
I remember you standing beside me there
And keeping those cattle away.

Yeah you turned out to be a pretty good mate
In our travellings down the track.
Even the times that I swore at you
—You never answered back.

And I remember that late night in Walgett,
The locals thought they'd have a go
And beat up an out-of-towner, eh,
And help themselves to me dough.

Well, your free-wheeling style of fighting
Had them scurrying off like mice!
By Jeez, I was glad of your company
Even though you bit me twice.

Yeah, you've turned out to be a pretty good mate
You stuck by me all through the years.
You've always been here to protect me
When I've had too many beers.

But at times you could be kind of stupid
Like right now with your leg in a trap.
And there's still three days walk to the next flamin' town
That I can't even find on a map.

I wish I could think of some other way.
I wish I could do something else instead.
But I can't sit here watching you suffer,
When with one bullet you'll be quickly dead.

Don't lie there expecting a miracle
With that trusting look in your eye.
I can't even give you a decent last meal,
All we've got is a tin of camp pie.

For God's sake, stop your looking at me
I'm finding it so hard to aim.
But it's the only thing I know of
That will give you an end to your pain.

Well, there you go, now I've done it
And I'll have to write down somehow
How two good mates came to be parted
And why you're resting peacefully now.

PART 3

BRAINPOWER

· *Dogs unafraid to use their intelligence*

ELEVATED TO THE PEERAGE

Jim Kelly, Naracoorte, South Australia

Our Prince Charles arrived on the same day in 1948 as his royal namesake. He was a fat and cuddly red kelpie pup with possibly a drop or two of dingo blood. If Charlie wasn't the pick of the litter, somebody else got an exceptional choice.

He learnt his name very quickly and was one of those amazing pups who seemed to know all he had to, right from the start. Except for the occasional ride in the old army surplus jeep, dogs had to do all their own footwork in those days. We always carried a stockwhip and galloped about a lot more than we do today. The young dog had no fear of the whip and seemed to develop a special relationship with Solo and Melody, the main stockhorses in our stable. On hot days, while our horses were tied up to the fence, he would stand in the horses' shadows, where the ground was cooler. In the middle of the day, this often meant lying under the tail of the horse, right next to the dangerous back hoofs.

As time went by, Charlie developed into the most outstanding dog of my life, both as a yard dog and as a paddock worker, with a big wide cast. He was a rarity in this age of specialisation of eye, bark and cast. He would work for any one of the family and as he grew older, was rarely tied up. We loved him with respect and admiration.

In the middle of the night in August 1955, when we had a team of Poll Shorthorn bulls on feed in the bull pens, I was awakened by Charlie barking at my bedroom window on the front verandah. We had a baby daughter in an adjoining room and were frightened the hullabaloo would wake up the rest of the household. I told Charlie in my gruffest, deepest, whisper to 'Go and lie down.'

To our surprise, he barked back. I said, 'Something must be wrong, he's trying to tell me something,' and leapt out of bed into a dressing gown. With a torch from the kitchen, I left the house by the back door. Charlie met me with a wagging tail as we walked down the path to the bull shed. As we got closer, I could hear banging, crashing and very heavy breathing. A gate had come open somehow and two bulls were fighting in a confined space. It was tricky and dangerous separating the heaving bodies and I expect Charlie barked and so distracted them long enough for me to push one through the gate and close the catch.

Prince Charles was a hero. The bruises to the bulls must have been superficial, as they won big ribbons at the Royal Adelaide Show a few weeks later.

I've spent my working life of some fifty years with animals. I've seen some remarkable behaviour where an individual has performed in special ways, either to solve a problem or bring attention to themselves, but always within the normal range of behaviour for its species. A cow that hides her calf, a draughthorse that pulls to the utmost of its strength, a sheep which always walks through a gate first so the mob follows.

They are displays of superior intelligence that make close contact with individual animals such a rewarding experience. But Charlie's behaviour that night was quite exceptional, outside the norm, even for a smart dog.

Consider his position. Somehow he became aware of the commotion going on in the bull shed. Perhaps he slept there, we don't know. Normal dog behaviour would have been to bark at the fighting bulls till something happened.

Charlie knew he could not fix the problem and must have known I could. When I scolded him for barking at the window, normal behaviour would have been to lower his tail and head and skulk away, yet he kept barking in a most defiant and unusual way, so that I got the message that he needed help. He kept the idea to deliver the message in his head, despite the scolding.

For me this was a unique experience that I have often contemplated. Down our way Charlie was almost elevated to the peerage, despite his colonial background. We addressed him, if time permitted, as Sir Charles.

NOT THE NEIGHBOUR'S SHEEP

Hurtle Baldock, Buckleboo, South Australia

Undoubtedly the best dog I owned was my first, when starting on a scrub block after the war. He was a black and tan named Tim and although a slow beginner, was uncanny.

At shearing or crutching time, if we missed any stragglers he would bring them in, even to the point of delivering them right to the back door of the shearing shed. While mustering in the scrub he would find sheep I didn't know were there.

One day my brother and I saw three sheep on their own a quarter of a mile away. I sent Tim to bring them in. After running some distance he stopped and refused to go around them. After three attempts to get him to bring them in, we went to investigate.

We were amazed to discover they were a neighbour's sheep, with only their brands and six months difference in wool growth to set them apart from our sheep. I told my brother the dog could read brands!

Many years later when his hearing and eyesight had failed, I had to put him down, so I shot him while he was alseep.

NIGHT MUSTER

Zita Ward, Singleton, New South Wales

The following episode is a tribute to a black kelpie sheepdog named Nigger. During the late 1930s we lived on a farm which was situated at the end of the road, and well off the beaten track. It was a valley with a creek which forked into three separate narrow valleys. Each valley was separated by high, and quite rugged, wooded hills, mostly unfenced.

It was a very pretty place, quiet and full of tranquillity—except for the dingos which seemed to have arrived en masse very soon after we stocked up with sheep. Their attacks on our flock became so bad we were forced to yard all the sheep each night.

This proved a difficult task for us with only my father to do it, plus help from my eleven year old brother and me, aged sixteen. We had several dogs who would work well for anyone, but Nigger was a new, young dog being trained by Dad, and not allowed to go with us kids.

One night my father was called away from home overnight, which left only the children to muster. Our mother arranged to do the valley near our house, and since she did not ride a horse it meant walking a few kilometres into the rough foothills. She decided to take Nigger with her, hoping he would understand her inadequate instructions, in place of Dad, who had a mighty voice and a whistle which carried a power of authority.

Just on dusk my brother and I arrived back at the house after yarding our mob, only to find our mother was not yet back. We rode up the valley to meet her and found that she had lost Nigger in the scrub. Obviously he had moved out of earshot as our calling and whistling failed to get a response.

By now it was quite dark. The area was so rugged and dangerous for anyone not very familiar with it that we were forced to give up and hope that Nigger could find his way back home. We had already lost a few dogs who had been enticed to follow the dingo pack and had never returned. Our father would be most upset if we lost Nigger as well.

About 9 pm we heard strange noises at the back gate of our house yard. There we found Nigger holding a small flock of about 50 sheep in a tight circle. This was an incredible feat for a lone dog to have shepherded his sheep out of that steep, rough country and several kilometres back to the house.

Nigger was quite knocked up and glad of a late feed. Needless to say we were overjoyed to have him back safely, and also to have the sheep safely home since more than likely they would have been victims of the wild dogs who persistently waited for a chance to maul any strays.

RED TED ALERT

Bruce Rodgers, Yeelanna, South Australia

When I came to this district 63 years ago, my nearest neighbour, P H (Mick) Wagner, had a sheepdog called Red Ted, which was from a red kelpie bitch by a border collie dog. Ted was a good all-round sheepdog, and had a lot of intelligence in matters other than working sheep.

We had a scrub block adjoining the Wagner farm, which had no improvements, and we were using Wagner's stable and horse yards, and camped in a hut near the sheds.

One night about midnight, Ted insisted on barking at Mick's back door, and would not stop when told. Then he went to the bedroom window and put his paws on the sill and barked more than ever.

Mick got out of bed and, armed with a hurricane lantern, went to investigate. The first thing he saw was his own two horses in the back garden, and he realised that our eight horses would not be far away. He found them beginning to tear open and eat some seed wheat which had been stacked in bags and pickled. Fortunately they had not eaten much, because a lot of pickled wheat would have killed them, and horses at that time were scarce and precious. My father said Ted was a very valuable dog and had probably saved us hundreds of pounds. We made sure the horse yards gate was closed correctly thereafter.

ONE YELL TOO MANY

Tresna Shorter, Katherine, Northern Territory

Despite his lack of training, Fella, being a border collie, had natural ability and knew instinctively what to do. This was more than could be said for the rest of us. My husband, who was more interested in wheat growing than dealing with animals, had little patience when it came to sheep.

In his impatience, it was not long before he started yelling at all of us for not being in the right place at the right time. I could take being yelled at a couple of times, but being a city girl and still learning country ways, I soon became annoyed. After all, I reasoned, we were helping him out during a labour shortage, weren't we? Where would he be without us? Foolishly, I expected gratitude, not abuse.

Eventually, he yelled at me one time too many and I turned around and started walking home. Next, he yelled at Fella, and to our amazement, Fella also turned and strutted home across the paddock with his crooked tail waving in the air.

Later, my husband had a good laugh that even the dog wouldn't put up with his rotten temper.

MY DOG ELS

Rob Williams, Albury, New South Wales

I won her in a pub at Blackall. She was mostly blue cattle plus something else. So that's what I called her—Els.

She was easy enough to train, but most of the time she'd do something else first. Being a patient sort of bloke, this didn't worry me too much.

I had two other dogs who were good workers and Els soon copied them. But she always included some other job as an extra. She believed she was a star. As it turned out, she was.

I got a job bringing down a small mob of cattle, all a bit rough, from Nardoo way, to Cloncurry. This is back in the fifties. The country was bloody dry and hot. Because I was broke, I took this on, on my own. Just three dogs, three horses and me. Any quids at the end were mine! I wasn't worried about condition. I was pushing them fast and me and my dogs really worked.

About two days run from the 'Curry, my horse Sampson caught his foot in a hole, fell with me pinned beneath him and he was trapped. I was too. I found out later that my leg was busted in two places and I was concussed.

I came out of it some time later with Sampson going wild every so often, two dogs sitting in some shade, but no bloody Els. She'd run off. I've had it, I thought.

Now this is what Els did. She ran all right—in a straight bloody line to the only two blokes within 50 miles. How she knew, I'll never know.

These blokes were fencing. They told me that this sweaty looking, tired dog came up, barking at them, and pulling at the pants of the bloke with the wire. He thought she was mad and hit her, but she kept circling, barking and running off. She did this four or five times.

In the bush, the real blokes get a feeling about things. I can't explain it. These blokes, God bless them, got that feeling. They got in their ute and followed her. It was only about six miles.

She led them back to me and I suppose that's the end of the story. Els should have looked after the cattle. She could have had a laze in the shade, but that dear, stupid bitch did something else—and saved my bloody life.

BLUEY WARNER

Mavis Taylor, Uranquinty, New South Wales

Bluey Warner, as the name implies, was a warner. If any stranger seemed the least bit aggressive, the dog would stroll over and take his heel gently in his mouth. But he had even more sense than that.

One day my two youngest girls went across to the neighbours' place to see their two mates. As with most children, they didn't use their heads. Away down to the creek they went to play in the water—a novelty as we hadn't had rain in ages. Typically, they just had to get in and get wet. The creek was fairly deep where they were and flowed into two dams before careering on down through our place.

Fred went out to milk, but Bluey Warner, who always had the herd waiting for him at milking time, wasn't there. This was so unusual, because you could nearly set the time by the dog. So Fred smelt trouble.

'Where are the girls?' he asked.

I told him they were over at the neighbours' place.

'Bluey Warner hasn't brought the cows in,' he said. 'Let's go.'

We went next door and told them the dog had not brought the cows in. And so the search was on.

Down at the creek we were met by four bedraggled children and a muddy dog coming up the track. They had climbed down into the creek and couldn't get out. The power of the rushing, rising water had been pushing them toward the dams. They had been four very frightened children on the brink of a tragedy.

They had called out, hoping to make someone hear up at the house. We lived about a half-mile from the creek and although we hadn't heard their calls, Bluey Warner had.

According to the eldest child, he turned up on the bank and they tried to get him to go for help. Instead, he crouched down and grabbed the eldest girl by her clothes and started pulling. This was enough to enable her to get a foothold in dry dirt and she scrambled out. She then lay down on the bank and pulled the other three out.

The children said Bluey Warner snarled and snapped at them. They couldn't believe his behaviour. We know dogs can't talk, but clearly they were getting a roasting from him, and a warning never to try playing in a swollen creek again.

READY TO STRIKE

Jeanette Osborne, Roadvale, Queensland

While Bluey and I were droving a herd of cattle along the road, one cow began to lag behind. I swung my whip, which promptly became stuck under my horse's tail.

When I had dismounted to retrieve the whip, my horse suddenly snorted and bolted. Spinning round, I came face to face with a huge brown snake rearing ready to strike me.

Bluey never hesitated. He charged in and tried to shake the snake to kill it. Instead he was bitten three times and died shortly afterwards. He had saved my life.

SHALLIE THE FAITHFUL

Tim Hardy, Penong, South Australia

It was just before shearing and Shallie, my six year old red kelpie bitch, and I had mustered up the wethers on the scrub block 30 miles from the house.

We had put them in a yard for the night before going home. At 6.30 next morning we left home in the ute to drive the sheep home. When we arrived at the yards we found that the sheep had broken out, so we scouted around in the vehicle and found them on the edge of the 3,000 acres of scrub. I let Shallie out to drive the sheep back to the yards through about one mile of scrub. While she was doing that, I went back to the yards to get a motorbike so I could go back and help her.

On my way back to her I hit a tree root and fell off the bike. I landed heavily on my back, hitting a stone. I couldn't move my body or legs. I realised my back was broken.

Shallie reached me after about half an hour. She drove the sheep around me, but sensed something was wrong so left the mob and came over to me. She licked my face and then lay down beside me. I dragged myself about 30 yards along a fence but couldn't go any further because the wire cut my hands. So I just settled down to wait for the family to come looking for me. I knew it would be ages because they would probably think I had dropped into the pub on my way home, or something like that.

I decided to write a note on a matchbox and then hooked it onto Shallie's collar. I told her to go home 30 miles away, but she wouldn't leave me. She just lay beside me all day from 9.30 in the morning until 9 o'clock at night, when finally a search party with a spotlight found me. The only way they could spot us was by picking up the shine of Shallie's eyes as she jumped up and down. An ambulance came and collected me, and Shallie was taken home.

Next morning, when my wife called Shallie, she wasn't there. She was found fifteen miles up the road on her way back to where she had been with me all day on the previous day.

While I was in hospital for three months learning to cope with life in a wheelchair, Shallie would not go near anyone, even for a pat. She must have been fretting. When I finally returned home, she went back to being her old self.

Since that accident three years ago she has retired from sheep work and spends all her time alongside my wheelchair.

OLD BILL

Gladys Maddison, Macksville, New South Wales

Old Bill, a black and tan kelpie, was about sixteen years old at the time of this incident.

I was bringing in a flock of young ewes with their first lambs and it was close to dusk. The gate was awkwardly placed and Rover, an untrained puppy, was overenthusiastic and separated one ewe from the flock. It careered down the paddock with Rover in full pursuit.

Meanwhile the ewes and lambs went quickly through the gateway with a little encouragement from Bill. I fastened the gate. Rover had returned, but when I looked around for Bill, he had disappeared, so I went off to look for the errant ewe.

It was nearly dark by now. I tried to get Rover to guide me to the ewe, but he didn't understand. The paddock was rough and boulder strewn, so it wasn't easy to find one missing ewe.

However, I heard a distant barking at intervals, then silence. I went down the gully in the direction of the barks. Rover left me and I followed him quickly, knowing he would lead me to Bill and, I hoped, the ewe.

Imagine my surprise when I reached the two dogs to find the ewe up to her neck in a waterhole that was only her length in diameter. She couldn't get out but there was old Bill at the side of the pool, hanging onto her wool with his teeth, letting go, barking to attract my attention, and grabbing her again so she wouldn't sink.

It was quite an effort to haul her out as she was in full wool and waterlogged. But all was well and after a short rest she went back up the hill to her baaing lamb.

It was all in a day's work for Bill. He retired a few years later as he was becoming deaf, but he lived to be 22 years old!

PART 4

A CUT
ABOVE THE REST

· *The champs*

NACOOMA GUS—A LEGEND IN HIS OWN LIFETIME

Lyndon Cooper, Kingston, SE South Australia

Over all the years I have been breeding and training working dogs, I have always found the true, all-round working dog the most fascinating and intelligent. He's the dog that can muster a paddock on his own, drive a mob of sheep to yards or homestead and also work in the yards when the mob has been yarded.

These dogs think for themselves. They seem to be able to work out where the stock has to go and they rarely get into trouble doing their work. Although I have great respect for a good yard dog, the all-rounder is the type of dog I enjoy breeding and working the most.

Nacooma Gus, my kelpie dog, a son of Bullenbong Mate, never ceases to amaze me with the level of intelligence he has. I remember one particular time a couple of years ago when I walked out from the homestead with Gus just on dusk. I cast him around a 60-acre paddock covered in thistles and dock to pick up a mob of 300 wethers that I had put in there a couple of days before to be drenched.

After about fifteen minutes, Gus returned without any sheep. I gave him some harsh words of advice and sent him out again to have another look. This time twenty minutes went by, but still no sheep and also no Gus. And it was getting quite dark. I returned home to collect the utility to look for the missing sheep and dog.

After driving around the paddock, I failed to find the sheep myself, so I headed for the gate into the next paddock which led into a laneway into the cattle yards. Much to my amazement, Gus and the 300 sheep were coming from the next 60-acre paddock into the laneway and out onto the track heading for home. Somehow the gate had been left open and the wethers had found their way into the next paddock.

Gus, obviously not being able to find any sheep in the first 60-acres, went through the fence and mustered the next paddock, found the sheep and knew where to take them to get them on the track for home.

At shearing time at our place there is always a lot of talk about dogs, some funny, some serious, but rarely does a shearer have to wait for sheep.

One year we had a new roustabout. He was fascinated with the dogs and the way they would cast out into the hills, muster a mob of sheep and bring them into the yards while we were working in the shed. Only on the very odd occasion would they leave one behind.

At about 11 am on the second-last day of shearing, the weather was looking rather threatening and one of the shearers suggested I bring the last mob in. As I was busy wool classing, I took Gus out into the paddock and cast him out over the bracken-covered hills, left him to it and returned to the shed to go on classing wool.

After about 30 minutes, much to the amazement of our bewildered roustabout, over the hill and into the yards came this mob of sheep.

During lunch it started to rain, so we pushed these sheep into the shed. It was chock-a-block full. You couldn't fit another sheep in, but we felt very pleased with ourselves as it rained all day.

As we walked from the shed after knock-off time, the roustabout spotted approximately twenty sheep up on top of one of the hills. He looked at me and said, 'What are those sheep up on the hill there, Coop? Gus never leaves any behind, eh?'

Thinking very quickly, I replied, 'Well, he knew they wouldn't fit in the shed, so he left those few behind.'

Well, I can tell you that roustabout was the best publicity officer I could ever have employed because various versions of this true story circulated the local hotels for some time.

I know a dog may not be that smart, but for a dog that has won four State Farm and Yard Dog Championships, been in 56 finals and won 24 of them, represented South Australia in the National Titles four times being placed as high as third, as well as learning tricks like climbing ladders and walking backwards, I reckon he's capable of almost anything.

THE TRIAL

Garry Somerville, Mosman, New South Wales

This story told to me about 35 years ago is based on fact, but I have changed the names.

Ben had spent all his life in the bush, mostly as a station hand, sometimes as a drover. He had wandered about central Queensland and western New South Wales, never staying long in one place.

At 75 years of age, he was a bachelor, in good health, a teetotaller, a non-smoker and had spent the last three years as station hand for Mr Alex Davidson on Burran Station, near Wilcannia.

A pillar of honesty who worked hard from dawn to dusk, he was an excellent sheepman who kept to himself. His sole companion was his eight year old red kelpie Sailor. A keen lover of dogs, Ben had acquired Sailor as a seven week old pup for five shillings from a passing traveller. He had taken a fancy to the pup and thought it a good 'un. His previous dog had died from distemper.

Ben was an expert with dogs, and had patiently trained Sailor over the years to be an exceptionally good sheepdog. During this time they had become inseparable and Ben had never missed an opportunity to correct or encourage his charge. The results had been amazing—the dog understood everything Ben said.

Sailor bedded down every night in the shearers' quarters alongside Ben, some distance from the homestead. It was common for Ben to chat away to Sailor for hours on end. They were truly great companions. Of all the dogs he had owned, Ben knew he had an extra soft spot for Sailor, though he never let on. Wherever he went, his four-footed friend was always within scent distance.

Ben's boss knew them both well and considered them worth three men. When a job had to be done, these two could be relied on.

One Sunday, he remarked casually to Ben, 'The sheepdog trials are on at the showground next Saturday. Do you want me to enter you and Sailor when I'm in town today?'

Ben, no lover of crowds, hesitated for a moment, then said, 'OK, we'll give it a go.'

For the rest of the week Ben gave Sailor a good work-out with the sheep whenever the opportunity arose. It was uncanny how they worked. Ben never stopped talking to the dog; it was as if each understood exactly the other's thoughts. The companionship and unity between them was unique.

Ben knew Sailor could do well at the trials. But, he also knew they were both slowing up and even the long trip into town would be an effort for them.

When Saturday arrived Ben was up early and finished his chores in time to fit the harness of the horse and trap which his boss had given him permission to use. Today, Sailor, who usually trotted behind, was allowed up alongside Ben.

The Wilcannia showground is huge, surrounded by a picket fence, and when Ben finally arrived, the ground was crowded, with some competitors having come from as far as 50 miles away. The sheepdog trials were a popular event and everyone made an effort to be there. The entrance fee was one pound, with the winner's purse twenty-five. There were twelve entrants and Sailor had drawn No. 12.

Each competitor started with 100 points, the judge deducting points when the dog made an error. The dog and handler started from a common peg and, on a signal from the judge, the dog would be cast out by the handler to the opposite end of the ground where three sheep were standing.

The dog had to bring the sheep back to the handler as quickly as possible. It then had to take the same sheep through a drafting race and some 200 yards to a small bridge. Finally it had to drive the sheep another 200 yards, then put them in a pen. The handler then shut the gate to conclude the competition. The maximum time allowed was fifteen minutes. Points were deducted for slow work, sheep being off course, dogs overrunning and sheep breaking away from the dog.

Ben chose a cool spot on the outskirts to park the trap so Sailor could rest up a bit, away from the crowd, as he waited his turn. Ben and Sailor kept to themselves, Ben nodding occasionally to someone he knew. Most of the other competitors and spectators congregated round the start. Ben knew Sailor would need all the rest he could get if he was to put up a good show, so he was content to watch from a distance.

Promptly at 11 am, the steward blew his whistle for the first contestant. The crowd was silent and each competitor stood at the starting peg. The first three dogs of mixed breed were average and scored between 80 and 90 points each. The fourth dog, a huge black and tan kelpie, was very good. He made few errors and his cast was as good as Ben had seen, and Ben had guessed correctly when the score went up at 95. 'A tough one to beat,' he muttered to Sailor, who was still asleep under the trap in the shade.

The day wore on. Two other dogs scored 91 and 92, the others in the eighties.

The ninth competitor was Floss, a well-bred two year old border collie with good markings. A good-looking dog Ben thought, and one he guessed would be difficult to beat.

He had heard of the collie's exploits at previous trials. Both he and his handler were well known and raised murmurs from the crowd from their bearing. The dog sat upright and willing, a good sign in trial competitions. Floss's cast and lift were neat and straight and the only fault, Ben thought, was that the young dog overran a little. A polished performer, Floss brought the three sheep straight down the middle of the ground.

At the first obstacle the collie was faultless, putting the sheep through the race perfectly with a maximum score. Ben admired this dog; he was certainly a champion. He had an air of confidence about him, and he reminded Ben of what Sailor had been like some six years ago. He looked at Sailor and smiled.

When 98 went up on the board there was a tremendous outbreak of cheering. Ben realised then what they were up against. This Floss was a good one, better than any he could recall. He roused Sailor just prior to their turn. 'You'll do your best, old boy,' he whispered as he walked towards the start.

When Ben and Sailor arrived at the peg, a quietness settled on the ground in deference to their age. Sailor, with his white whiskers and muzzle, and Ben, stooped over slightly, were a direct contrast to the collie, Floss, and his handler.

Sailor sat quietly at the start till the three sheep were liberated at the other end of the ground. When they were standing steady, the judge signalled the timekeeper and Ben was given the signal to start. For about ten seconds, Ben hesitated so that Sailor could get the scent. This was going to be a tough one, Ben knew.

Suddenly there was a change in Sailor. He sat upright, listening with his ear back in an antenna fashion. Ben cast him out: 'Go way back, boy!'

Sailor, sensing he had to do well, was off like a flash and Ben, because of the obstacles, used a shrill whistle to guide him. It was a perfect pear-shaped cast and he came up smartly behind the sheep and, on Ben's whistle, halted directly behind them.

Sailor, as if by telepathy, delivered the sheep without fault in a straight line down the centre of the field. He was precise and neat, handling them quietly but with assurance. Never for a second did he give them the opportunity to be contrary. He was indeed master of the situation, and Ben knew Sailor had gained the maximum points for his effort.

Ben's hands began to sweat. Though excited, he kept a poker face.

Next Ben led the way round the fence with the three sheep behind him and Sailor taking up the rear. On reaching the drafting race Ben stepped into the car tyre placed on the field for the handler, who has to stay there till the sheep are put through the race by the dog. Until now Sailor had not made a mistake, but just as the last sheep was about to go through the race he veered a fraction to the right. It was only for a second, but Ben knew they had lost vital points.

From the time Sailor left the starting peg Ben had talked to him constantly, giving him encouragement and commands, and trying to keep one guess ahead of his dog.

After the race it was 200 yards to the next obstacle, the bridge. Ben encouraged Sailor by talking to him reassuringly; again, he could not fault his dog's effort. Once more he realised they had gained maximum points. He was at work on the sheep immediately the last one left the bridge.

With the final obstacle, the pen, some 200 yards ahead, Ben told Sailor, 'Good boy!'

There was, unknown to Ben, whose full concentration was on his dog, a silence around the ground as everyone sensed the closeness of the scores.

'Go back, go way fore, go back.' Sailor appeared to be on a string; everything Ben said, the dog did.

With the three sheep close by the pen and Sailor glued with his nose twitching in front of them, one paw raised as if to pounce, excitement reached its peak. Two sheep raced into the pen, with a slight movement from Sailor. One to go! Suddenly, for no apparent reason, the remaining sheep ducked out of the edge of the wing. Sailor had him back and in the pen in almost the same instant, but

Ben knew as he moved to close the pen that he had lost another point.

The crowd cheered and everyone except Ben and Sailor seemed to go mad. Ben returned slowly to his trap and quietly fondled Sailor's ear. 'You went close, boy. It was a fine effort.'

When the score of 97 was marked up, a ripple again went round the crowd. Floss had won by one point. No-one had dreamed that any other dog would come near to Floss's score. However, Ben's experience told him the younger dog had deserved his win, so he tried not to let Sailor sense his disappointment.

Floss's owner, knowing how close the result had been, finally broke away from his friends and walked over to congratulate Ben on the fine performance Sailor had put up. He, too, recognised a good dog when he saw one.

He was there some minutes with Ben, and when he returned to his friends he had a worried look and seemed at a loss for words. One of his friends joked, 'What's the matter, Alf? Anyone would think you'd lost!'

He didn't reply for some time. When he did, his voice shook. 'You saw how that old kelpie worked those sheep so close ... do you know he's been totally blind for two years?'

STILL A CHAMPION

Allan & Annica Sutherland, Ballidu, Western Australia

Tessie was the typical retired sheepdog enjoying her last years with the luxury of little work and plenty of good food.

In her heyday, Tessie, a border collie, had been a successful trial dog in Western Australia. Eventually she had to be retired from trialling as she cunningly began to use her intelligence to escape discipline when competing. We would like to share a story from the time when she had become known as Old Tessie.

It was a chilly, moonlit winter night during seeding. A gate had been left open and the sheep, being sheep, had made their way out. Frank, the boss, had set out in pursuit with the eager old dog on the back of the ute. He returned some time later with neither sheep nor dog.

Meanwhile Allan had set out on the motorbike to help. After an hour of fruitless searching, he also gave up and returned the bike to the shed. As he headed back to the house he heard the twang of the fence as Tessie streaked through.

Allan was surprised to find Old Tessie had beaten him home with the sheep and was holding the mob at the gate of the house yard. Tessie had driven the mob of approximately 600 sheep for two or three kilometres.

Only days before this event, we had been considering putting Old Tessie to rest as her age seemed to be catching up with her and her health was declining. This display proved Old Tessie still had plenty of life in her.

SECOND IN COMMAND TO BULLENBONG MATE

Nancy Withers, Naracoorte, South Australia

Before I had Mate I did not realise the things a working dog could do above the normal everyday ones. Mate educated many people who had worked with stock all their lives. He was truly an incredible animal and, although I have had many good dogs and some which come close, I doubt I'll ever see his like again. The trouble is that you can't obtain kelpies of pure old blood any more and a lot of them have been crossed with dogs of much less talent by breeders who don't understand them.

For the eight and a half years that we lived between Robe and Kingston, I did all the stockwork with the help of a station hand. We ran 1,000 cattle and 7,000 sheep. Most of the work was done on horses and the country was pretty rough. Without Mate and his offspring, I simply could not have managed. Tim, my husband, was constantly busy clearing scrub, fencing, sowing pasture and eradicating rabbits and weeds.

Mate was the foundation of my business. He introduced me to many new friends and my sport of yard trialling, which has taken me to many places. I became fascinated with the study of the genetics of the working kelpie and spent many hours learning where particular traits came from.

All my stud dogs are Mate's descendants. I am not ashamed to admit that a dog changed my life. This is how it all started.

A well-known kelpie breeder and friend of mine from New South Wales rang one evening and, after the usual chitchat, he asked if I would be interested in a seventeen month old kelpie dog which he had bred and an elderly man had reared for him.

My friend had recently suffered a very nasty back injury in a fall from a horse and was unable to work the dog and felt he would be wasted.

'He's not a bad-looking dog,' he said. 'Knows a bit, too. Could do your stud a bit of good. He's all sound old blood.'

Although the dog had never seen a sheep and I already had a potential sire, I decided to take him. His name was Bullenbong Mate, Mate for short.

He was despatched by train and arrived four days later. I first saw him in a large crate. He was a big, black and tan kelpie dog with a broad head and the darkest of chestnut tan markings. 'Hello there! You must be Mate,' I said.

There was no reply. Not a wag of the tail, not an inclination of the head. He just stood and looked back at me with as much pride as I've ever seen in an animal. And that was to characterise our relationship over the years. He was arrogant, proud and supremely sure of himself. An aristocrat.

Despite his four days' travelling, he was still shiny black. He was of medium to large frame with strong, although not overly heavy, bone. However, he had quite a short, straight tail.

We loaded Mate into the hatchback part of the car, and headed for home. Mate rested his broad head on the back of the rear seat and as I drove I glanced in the rearview mirror to see him looking in my direction. I said to my friend, 'You know, I think I'm going to like this dog.' Almost as I finished speaking Mate gave one deep 'woof'. We all burst out laughing.

So began the best relationship I have ever had with an animal. I have worked with animals most of my life and as a breeder and trainer of dogs I have handled hundreds, but Mate stands alone as the greatest animal I have ever had the pleasure of working with. When I write or speak of him, I claim no credit for his ability. He was an extremely well-bred dog, with some excellent station and trial dogs in his pedigree, well-proven sires and dams. In fact, Mate taught me more about shepherding sheep than I ever could have taught him.

Quietly intelligent and with that immense pride, he was a gentle and affectionate dog. However, he was difficult to work. He liked to think for himself and had an incredible memory. Those who worked with him, people and dogs alike, were left in no doubt as to his own opinion of his status—he was the best dog around and he was invincible.

For the first few months, I tried to instil some discipline. This proved a frustrating and exhausting task for both of us. All the positive commands were fine. It was things like 'come', meaning 'come straight away', which seemed to fall on selectively deaf ears. All the more annoying because he wasn't rushing off anywhere but merely proceeding in the opposite direction at his own steady pace. He absolutely refused to 'sit' and after many hours of anguish I settled for 'stop', which I persuaded myself had the same effect and even prided myself that he obeyed this command about 80 per cent of the time.

I could tell many stories about his cleverness finding and driving sheep in rough country, his fearlessness in the yards and his sense of humour, but if I had to tell just one, this would be it.

The first indication that all was not well with Mate, now three years old, was when he refused to eat, first one day, then another. We were busy crutching at the time and although I was concerned, this was somewhat allayed by the fact that Mate was quite happy to proceed with mustering and yard work. However, when he didn't eat for the third day and I noticed that he wanted to, but appeared uncertain to do so, I took him to the local vet straightaway.

The vet took his temperature and then examined him, pressing his abdomen firmly, but the dog did not flinch. It was decided to put him on medication and we proceeded home.

After two days he had not improved and was visibly losing weight. Once again, it was off to the vet and another examination. Once again, we arrived home with medication. At lunchtime, I received a call from my husband's nephew, Chris, who managed a nearby property. He was also crutching and had four crossbred ewes with half-grown lambs at foot which kept eluding the muster and escaping into a patch of thick scrub.

'Could you please bring Mate,' was the request. 'They're pretty tough and cunning and he's the only chance I have of getting them.'

I explained that Mate was ill, but agreed to do it, thinking I would carry Mate to the edge of the scrub and then let him go. At least he wouldn't have to run to get there. So off we went and after catching and saddling the horses, I mounted and Chris lifted Mate up to me where he sat in his favoured position in front of me in the saddle with his front paws braced against the horse's neck.

We found the ewes and lambs at the edge of the scrub and they shot away into it. Before I could lift him down, Mate leapt from the horse and was after them. The scrub was so thick that it was very difficult to walk through. Chris and I stopped at the edge of the scrub and waited. Soon the sheep appeared and were milling near our feet. Suddenly one ewe sat down, then another, heads stretched out flat on the ground in front of them.

'This is typical,' said Chris. 'Turn your back and they'll be off into the scrub as quick as a flash.'

We decided to tie the legs of the ewes which were down and did this as Mate held the other sheep. In the meantime, another ewe lay down and suddenly the one still standing bolted straight over Mate, knocking him aside in his attempt to stop her. He disappeared after her and the lambs took off in another direction. Muttering our disgust, we tied the other ewe and shortly Mate brought the last ewe back. He backed her the last few metres until Chris grabbed her. Then Mate turned and disappeared back into the scrub. Ten or more minutes later, he appeared with the four flighty lambs under control. He held them while we caught them and tied their legs. We left them to be collected by the four-wheel drive.

When Mate and I arrived home I offered him a drink. He wanted one but seemed too apprehensive to do so. I knelt down beside him and tried to coax him to take some water. He sat down alongside me, looked into my eyes, reached out with his paw and touched me gently on the arm. That was it! He was asking for help and I had to do something.

I rang a vet in Mt Gambier for his opinion and it was decided that I should take Mate there immediately to be examined. An operation was duly planned for first thing in the morning.

The dog was found to have had a blocked bowel, an extremely painful condition, which the vet said could normally be picked up in two days. Mate, however, so arrogant, so proud and so stoic, had worked every day and eaten nothing for nearly a week. I felt terrible that I had allowed him to work. Then I thought of Mate's ego and knew he would never have stood for not working without getting very upset in his kennel.

Mate hovered near death for several days. He was fed intravenously. On the fifth day after the operation, Mate could hold his head up and at last I knew he would survive. However, he was literally a skeleton with a starey black and tan coat. The hair was beginning to lift from his ears.

As usual, that afternoon, we headed off to the vet's for his intravenous feed. Chris had phoned to ask me to bring him something he wished to borrow on my way to town and, with Mate lying in the hatchback rear of my car, I pulled up near Chris's shearing shed. Chris and his dogs were working sheep in the yards and the dogs were barking as they forced the sheep into the race. I got out leaving one of the doors open and walked about 25 metres from the car.

Suddenly, Chris called out, 'Have a look behind you!'

I turned to see Mate coming towards the yards. He had dragged himself over the back of the rear seat, between the front seats and out the door. In doing so, he had reopened the cut in his side. As he came towards me he staggered and fell. Fluid trickled from his wound. He picked himself up again, moved a few drunken steps, staggered and fell as I reached him. Tears welled up in my eyes as I held him. Mate was *the* best dog in the district and *he* was coming to work.

It was three weeks before Mate was able to drink milk and another week before he could eat meat. Six weeks after the operation he started to improve.

Mate worked the stock on our property in South Australia for seven years. He also worked in the hills of the Great Dividing Range in New South Wales, the Riverina, steep river frontage country in Victoria and on several properties in South Australia.

We competed in yard trials in three States and he was placed in five State Championships. His descendants are worked in most States of Australia, and some work in Scandinavia.

Although Mate was a champion in the yards, in my opinion it was in the paddock, mustering rough country and shepherding sheep, where he truly excelled. He require very little guidance from me and often spent a great deal of time searching and mustering out of sight. His uncanny ability intrigued me and I quickly learned to give him a go and be patient when things were difficult.

ROCKETED TO STARDOM

Shirley Hands, Boyup Brook, Western Australia

After three weeks of shearing we felt a sense of release when the sheep were all mustered and the last day of shearing arrived. I felt thankful that the discipline of shearers' hours was almost over when I took that morning's smoko into the shed. I had no sooner put the food down on the side table than the boss looked over from the wool press and said, 'How about getting the straggler ewe out of the oat crop?'

Besides being the cook and 'bottlewasher', I seemed to be expected to be responsible for the mustering—although no-one formally said so. The crossbred ewe had never been called 'a straggler' before. She was a very old target. Each member of the household, from the boss downwards, had tried to muster her, but she and her two lambs had evaded us all winter.

She had been the subject of several dinner table mutterings along the lines of, 'I'll shoot the old sod'. All attempts to get her had failed and she still lurked in the 100-acre paddock where the crop was growing—about a mile from the shed. The oats, just coming into head, looked like an impenetrable green fortress.

I felt the task was hopeless, particularly when I looked at my youthful companion, a small black bitch with a sharp inquisitive face, pointed ears very wide at the base, four white feet and bronze markings around her smile.

Sunny, then a year old, had only begun her training at the onset of shearing, but she showed a lot of promise mustering chooks and had a keen eye.

With Sunny beside me I opened the gates into the yards and walked through five acres of bushland, and crossed the gully and hill before opening the gate into the crop. After half circuiting the paddock to the far side of the crop, I saw the cunning old girl, grazing quietly on the grass by the fence on the edge of the crop. Sunny, walking by my side, tensed as she saw her quarry.

Her eyes homed in on the ewe who looked up and saw us. She ignored our advance until we were within 200 metres of her then, gathering up her burly lambs, she set off at a smart canter along the firebreak.

As Sunny raced past them in a wide arc, intending to head them off, the ewe turned and, with her lambs, darted into the crop. Sunny, now only a metre in their wake, followed them. Ewe, lambs and Sunny vanished without a sound into the green forest. Their tracks were barely visible as the oats closed over their path.

Their sudden disappearance alarmed me. The crop stood five feet high, a green wall of stiff resistant stems. I hurried along the edge of the crop, calling Sunny to heel. As I stopped at intervals to wait and listen, a terrible sense of foreboding overcame me. What if I never found Sunny? Lost and blinded in that terrible green maze she could lie down from exhaustion and die. How could we ever get her out? I ran along the firebreak, panting and calling. It was nearing midday and I had to leave to do lunch for the shearers.

When I reached the shed with the food in the esky, the shearers and staff were all collapsed on the floor as though lunch was finished.

I told them the terrible reason for being late, of losing my precious dog in the oat crop. After they wolfed down the lunch they all consoled me, promising that when they had shorn the last sheep they would come and help look for her.

After lunch we went into the yards to shed the last batch of sheep. Within the open gate of the entrance yard was Sunny, standing modestly behind her quarry. The crossbred ewe was cowed and beaten and her two burly lambs were somewhat less jaunty than before.

Sunny spent a successful and happy life demonstrating the techniques of timing and movement, but her mastery over the old ewe had rocketed her to stardom. From that day on she became top dog and sat beside the boss in the front seat of the ute.

PERCY

Bruce Rodgers, Merriwa, New South Wales

Percy was an orphan pup that Bob Telfer had reared on a bottle. Bob turned up at our place with him one day. 'Dog's name is Percy,' Bob said. 'Might be OK. Give him a go.'

Percy was starey-eyed, black and tan and gangling.

He soon shone as a lead dog and then developed other skills that found him half a mile from the mob with a handful of stragglers, or right behind you at a gateway when a push was needed. He could handle cattle as well as sheep, and I wouldn't have a dog any other way.

On the particular night when Percy showed just how good he was, there was no moon. The plains grass was as high as a man standing and the three of us, a truck driver, my wife and I, were straining our ears to hear the slightest sound of 40 Angus weaner cattle lost off a truck from Casino that had arrived around midnight. The truck driver had rushed up to our door, out of breath and out of sorts.

'The weaners are all out,' he said. 'Someone must have left the back gate of the yards open and I didn't shut the front gate as I reckoned I'd only be twenty minutes.'

On with the boots, out with the torches, off with Percy and into the ute. We blocked half the mob in the lane, but 40 had managed to beat us onto the reserve, which was three miles long and a mile wide, with four roads out of it. The furthest they could go was probably Cassilis, 26 miles on a main road west. The thought paled me.

I told Percy to hop out of the back of the ute, and cast him in the general direction of west and hoped for the best.

The driver grew more and more agitated that there was no sight or sound of the cattle for half an hour or more.

Forcing my way through plains grass, falling over stones and logs, I headed for the fence on the far side. Every now and then I could hear something, but nothing that gave me a bearing. After half an hour of this, I was ready to give up until daylight. The night was black and so were the cattle.

Then suddenly I heard them coming down the fence heading east. Bobbing down, I tried to get a count of their backs on the dull skyline. Missing the count but knowing there was a good number, I blessed my luck and followed. Luck had nothing to do with it. Old Percy was bringing them along alone and unassisted.

When they reached the crossroad, they had drawn too far away for me to give him any orders. He had more idea than I where home was, but he had to cross them over the east-west highway on a long weekend.

Heart in my mouth, and catching up with my wife, neither of us knew where Percy was or where he was heading. The sound of late night traffic on the road sent chills down our spines.

We reached the road to find no cattle and no dog. Venturing on up the lane that leads to the front gate, there was Percy—just floating along behind the weaners. If he could talk, he would have said, 'Where have you all been?'

The truck driver was ecstatic. 'That must be the best dog in the world,' he said.

'Could be,' I replied. 'I'm going to teach him to shut gates next.'

PART 5

MIND-READERS

- *Perception*
- *A bit of ESP*

THE
MIND-READER

Tim Catling, Katanning, Western Australia

Scampy was a big, strong black dog that I owned in the late 1950s, or perhaps he owned me as I am sure he believed. He was a wonderful worker as well as a good mate. Sadly he was killed in his prime by a full drum of petrol being pushed off a truck.

He had one unusual trait, that of a mind-reader. In those days of farmers' first affluence for almost 30 years, all companies seemed to have travelling salesmen doing the rounds in the bush. My farm is split by the main road and most weeks two or three of these hopefuls would appear. Many were interesting people, but some only wasted one's time. It was this last group that Scampy seemed to be the mind-reader about.

If ever I was standing there wishing to myself that a particular salesman would leave, Scampy would always come along and pee on his trouser leg. This always had the desired result of the fellow leaving, usually quickly. How that dog knew I wanted the fellow to leave I never discovered, but he saved me many a boring time by this mind-reading.

I DREAMED
NOT OF GENIE

C McConnel, Esk, Queensland

I had wanted a working dog of my own ever since I left school, and finally Dad thought I knew enough to train a pup. I had visions of a red kelpie pup, but fate has a funny way of doing things. A friend who bred kelpies told Dad he had a pup that would suit me as she was too timid for a man. She had been sold as a small pup but had just been returned as being useless.

I wasn't too impressed when I went to collect my dream dog as she had to be dragged out of her kennel. She was an odd grey and tan colour. Anyway, I was told that if she didn't work out I could have a pup from the next litter, so Genie came home with me. I called her Genie hoping that she would turn out to be just like her namesake and solve all my problems.

Actually, I think she created more havoc than any other dog on the place. Nevertheless, she turned out to be a wonderful old character, never a top dog, but a handy old dog and as loyal to me as could be, even if she had to break the rules.

For instance, dogs were not allowed in the homestead garden. I was sick at the time with some wog or other and had had two days in bed. I heard Dad calling Genie to tie her up, and finally he came in and told me not to worry—but that she had been missing for the past two days.

Just then we heard a slight thumping from under the bed. Looking under we saw old Genie. Somehow she had got into the garden and then crept into the house and under my bed. It must have been terrifying for the silly old thing—but she was looking after me.

PREDICTING HIS RETURN

Margaret Shine, Pigeon Ponds, Victoria

Nigger was a small black kelpie with long hair who was very devoted to my husband, Doug. Often when he was walking along, Nigger would be that close behind him that he would get clipped on the jaw with his boot—but he would still stay there.

At shearing times I used to do the mustering on a horse. Sometimes Nigger would come all the way to the particular mob of sheep I was to bring back. Most times, however, he would only go through a couple of paddocks and while I was opening the gate, he would be gone, back to the woolshed and his master.

Doug would realise he had left, so would send him back to help me. Nigger would find me all right, often a long way from where he'd left me, and he would stay till we returned with the sheep. When we got about 200 yards from the sheep yards, he would run into the shed and sit at Doug's feet, so Doug would have to come and yard the sheep.

Nigger used to have a kennel in view of our kitchen window. When it was lunchtime, he would give a couple of sharp barks as he watched up the road. I knew I could then dish up because Doug would be home in about five minutes. We thought it was just because he had much better hearing than we had.

However, when Doug went fishing up on the Murray River near Robinvale, or to the Coorong in South Australia, he would be away for a week or ten days, and sometimes longer depending on the weather and the amount of fish he caught.

Doug never phoned to say when he would be back but Nigger always seemed to know the day he would be returning. He would be out of the kennel, give a couple of sharp barks, run around for a while, then settle down for half an hour or so. Then he would start the routine again.

When the children came home from school I would tell them Dad would be home that day. 'Watch Nigger,' I'd say. I could have bet the farm on him. Doug would come home some time late afternoon or even 10 o'clock at night.

Nigger certainly couldn't have heard the ute in the early morning when he started his barking and running.

At first Doug and the children didn't believe me, but as the years went on, Nigger's perception never let him or me down. It was a sad day for all of us when we lost him. I guess a dog like that you are lucky to have known, and to have owned, once in a lifetime.

PIP, THE MARRIAGE BROKER

Susan Martel, Gollan, New South Wales

My childhood memories of Pip are of an aged brown kelpie. Yet it is to Pip I owe my existence. It was he who sealed my parents' relationship.

Pip was my father's favourite dog. Dad, a young bachelor manager, had obtained Pip as soon as he returned from active duties in World War II. Pip was his mate and worked with him through drought, flood and ordinary times.

Mother, a tall, dark-haired, attractive young lady, was swept off her feet at the local Bachelors and Spinsters Ball by the handsome manager who, at 33, had somehow managed to avoid matrimony.

As young men of the land do, Dad had taken Pip when courting Mother, who worked at her father's stock and station agency. I often wonder what Mother thought of this since, as I remember, she did not appear to be over fond of dogs. I recall that she wouldn't let us bring the dogs into the house, take them in the car or even allow them into the garden. Yet when family discussions turned to the worth of dogs, even Mum would become a little misty-eyed when Pip was remembered.

It was not until my parents' fortieth wedding anniversary three years ago that I learnt why Pip was such a popular dog. Dad related the story.

One morning at the property where he worked, some 30 miles from town, he came out to discover that Pip was nowhere to be seen. All staff were alerted to keep an eye out for Pip, since dogs die quickly from snakebite.

That night, Dad received a phone call. Pip had turned up at Mother's family home. What a good excuse to go to town! Dad happily drove the 30 miles of potholed road to retrieve Pip.

He seemed to be convinced that for Pip to walk 30 miles, he must have been trying to drop some hint about the stock agent's beautiful daughter. So Dad did the only sensible thing and asked for Mother's hand, there and then.

GINGER

Helen Best, Barraba, New South Wales

We had a regular shearer, John, who was a friend of the family. He always brought his dog Ginger with him while he was at our shed for the weeks of shearing.

After several years of shearing and crutching, Ginger was a welcome addition to our workforce and Dad began to rely on him being there.

One year, a few days after our shed cut out, we were surprised to see Ginger on the doorstep and ready for work. He had found his way back to Fairview, seven miles from the town, on his own.

On the Friday night there was no sign of our extra dog. He had gone home to be with his owner.

Thus the pattern was set. Whenever John went to a big shed and left the dog in town, Ginger came out to Fairview and worked happily with us. He always only stayed until his owner returned to town, be it Friday night, or because of a break in routine because of rain and wet sheep. Ginger always knew.

As 'our' dog grew older, the seven miles seemed to be too much for him, so he made the decision to make his home permanently at Fairview.

However, we never did know how Ginger could possibly have known when John got back to town. Did he sense it, or did he pick up the sound of his car?

SO SHE WOULDN'T BE LEFT BEHIND

G H Harkin, Halifax, Queensland

My father was a drover from 1910 till late 1960. He had numerous stories of working dogs, the kelpie breed mostly, as they were the dogs that knew the job well, were very hardy, reliable, intelligent and obedient to the drover's command.

He had been camped for a while between jobs. The red kelpie bitch had produced puppies and kept them near a tree, some way from the camp. The time came when Dad had to move off to pick up his next flock of sheep. He started to pack up and harness his horses.

Suddenly he noticed a small puppy on the track to the bitch's tree. He picked it up and returned it to the tree, but found that others were missing.

The dog apparently had noticed the movements in the camp signalling they would soon be off. She had taken it upon herself to load her puppies into a wire basket under the wagon—the usual place for pups when the droving outfit was on the move.

HE KNEW THE TIME

Lynette Pouliot, Horsham, Victoria

Tim was bought from the Horsham Saleyards back in 1962 for the princely sum of £2 17s 6d. Although only three months old, he was alert and easy to handle and it was obvious that our new black and tan kelpie had loads of potential.

It wasn't long before he was displaying the qualities of zeal, stamina, intelligence and loyalty which characterise the Australian working dog. During his ten years of working with sheep, Tim literally 'never missed a beat', his energy never waned and he didn't take one 'sickie'.

As a stock agent, my husband inevitably had various moves around Victoria, the first being from Horsham to Ouyen. On the day of our departure Tim went missing, only to be discovered several hours later sitting up in the cabin of the furniture van. This had necessitated jumping at least seven feet from the ground through a half-open window—no mean achievement—but he wasn't going to be left behind!

Summertime in the Mallee often meant working in extreme heat. This, coupled with harsh ground conditions, did not slow up our dog at any time. He worked tirelessly and unerringly, whatever the task.

The big monthly sheep market in Ouyen made for a long and busy day. Tim had a routine from which he never deviated. He went about his work in the saleyards from daybreak until 2 pm, which was when selling commenced. At that time, he would sign himself off, come home for a rest and later have his tea.

On the dot of 5 pm he would be gone again, back to my husband. Instinctively he knew this was the time to start droving sheep up to the railway trucking yards.

We never worked out how he told the time so accurately!

UNDERSTOOD EVERY WORD WE SAID

L Lee Buckman, Gilgandra, New South Wales

We had never given much thought to retiring, but after receiving a good offer for the farm we decided maybe the time had come to go. Our only problem was what we should do with our dearly loved sheepdog and constant companion, Bill.

He was twelve years old and a bit old to start life again with a new boss, but was still very alert and agile. We wondered how he would adjust to life on the coast far away from sheep and the wide open spaces.

After the sale was completed we kept our sheep till within a few weeks of moving and then contacted our agent about selling them. The day the buyer came Bill did his job helping us to bring the sheep up to the yards and then he lay down in his usual place near the gate while we discussed prices and trucking arrangements. The buyer would be back for the sheep in two days.

The next morning Bill seemed very listless and just lay around in the shade. That night he wasn't even interested in his food, so we took him to his usual place in the header shed to sleep.

We had to bring the sheep up to the yards the next morning to load them up for their trip to their new home, but Bill just refused to come with us. Thinking he might be sick, we didn't worry him and got the sheep up without his help.

By lunchtime they had all been loaded with the help of the buyer's dogs and we waved them farewell and returned to the house to check how Bill was. He was dead.

We always said he understood every word we said, so perhaps he realised his work was finished and we didn't need him any more.

Bill's boss, my husband, died four years later. He missed the sheep and the wide open spaces. Retirement wasn't for him either.

SAM KNEW

R D McDonald, Kerang, Victoria

I feel I should not let the chance go by without telling this story of Sam. Now, I am not a writer or storyteller by nature, but I will put the true facts on paper and I think that should be of interest to many people.

Very early in the Dirty Thirties Depression, three young men decided to get out of Melbourne with all its troubles. One of these young men had worked in our district, so they made it their destination. They bought a horse and buggy which were very cheap in those days and off they set, seeking casual work and food as they travelled north.

One landowner gave them a dog for company. This was fine until they passed a paddock with sheep near the fence. The dog straightaway went quietly around the sheep and herded them to the roadside in quite good style. The dog kept doing the same thing each time they were near sheep.

The upshot was, when they reached our area, we were shearing and they did some casual work around the shed. I took notice of the dog and was impressed by his ability. I eventually offered them five pounds for the dog and they were delighted as five pounds was a lot of money in 1931.

The spokesman for the three was Sam Pelling, so I named the dog Sam. Then his real work began. We quickly became attached and he would not let me out of his sight.

We had a property 30 miles away from the home property and I used to do most of the sheep work there. To muster this property meant riding the 30 miles with Sam trotting along at the horse's heels. Sam then would muster and help draft the sheep, never turning a hair. If necessary, he would follow me home that evening. He was truly a great working dog and he loved it.

However, there were plenty of good working dogs. The real part of the story is as follows.

As you know, the war broke out on September 1939. I immediately joined the forces. I went into camp on October 1939, which meant that I had to place Sam in good hands. My elder brother gladly took care of him.

Knowing that Sam was very much a one-man dog, my brother kept him well tied up until he got a little bit settled before taking him around the sheep. Sam gradually adapted and seemed to like his new environment.

I was away for nearly three years from when I first took Sam to my brother. Sam by this time was quite at home there.

After returning from the Middle East, we got a few days' leave to go home. I arrived home late one Friday night and after greeting my family I enjoyed the strange feeling of a comfortable bed.

I woke early in the morning and was anxious to get out and look around. When I opened the back door, there was Sam on the mat. He looked at me a little guiltily, but as soon as I spoke and patted him, he was all over me, and until I delivered him back to my brother, he was glued to my heels.

To get to our place, Sam would have had to travel nearly 40 miles if he'd followed the roads. If he'd gone as the crow flies, it was at least 25 miles and he would have had to swim two major streams —the Murray and the Little Murray—and go through heavy red gum forests.

This was quite an achievement, apart from the timing of it all. It made me wonder if he had been uneasy when we were pinned down by shellfire in the desert, or bombed and strafed at.

I know I probably haven't told this very well, but now I feel too sentimental to rewrite it or say any more.

PART 6

WHOOPS!

· *Heart in the right place, but sometimes that's not enough!*

THE INDISCRETIONS OF PETE THE PUP

John Sykes, Bordertown, South Australia

Pete the Pup was born of quite common parentage. His father belonged to our southern neighbour, his mother to our eastern neighbour.

Within a few years Pete the Pup knew the entire layout of the farm, knew where the gates were and, more importantly, the nature of Dad's way of doing things. This was supplemented by the way he understood my mother's soft touch. On returning from a hard few hours' work, he would always line up for a leftover chop bone or a piece of cake for morning tea.

I found out one day just how human a nature Pete the Pup had. It was at shearing time. It was hot and I was putting sheep in the shed, running them up the platform. I wasn't getting on terribly well. Sweat was flowing and my blood pressure was rising. I was standing at the bottom of the ramp waving my arms and generally shouting at the sheep.

Suddenly I felt a large grab on my ankle and, looking down, I noticed Pete the Pup just pulling his head out from between the rails. He was peering up at me. In his eagerness to move the sheep up the ramp, he had given one just a little nip on the leg to encourage them, nothing drastic, but just enough to get them going. Well! On this particular occasion, he had grabbed my ankle and when I looked down in amazement at him, the look on his face was most expressive. It said, 'I am so sorry, boss. I got the wrong leg. I didn't mean it. I just got the wrong leg.' He looked terribly apologetic.

Perhaps the greatest indiscretion was the day one of my sisters' future in-laws came to stay with Mum and Dad for a weekend. They had never met my parents and arrived on the Saturday morning from Melbourne in a large, white Mercedes.

Mum and Dad walked out to the car and while they were opening the door to allow the future mother-in-law out, Pete the Pup came to inspect.

My father was introduced to her by my sister and while they were shaking hands, Pete the Pup calmly walked between them and, lifting his leg, widdled down the future mother-in-law's stockinged leg. My father was extremely embarrassed, my sister was horrified and Pete the Pup had rather a sore backside for a few days.

BAILED UP

Tom Hordacre, Tenterden, Western Australia

This happened during the 1930s when I was a schoolboy.

The annual Christmas Tree at the Tenterden Hall was always a big event for the local children. A nearby farmer was to be Father Christmas. My father, being the proud owner of a model T Ford, would pick the old chap up at a prearranged point, close to his home.

The appointment was kept by my father. After a few minutes' wait, and no sign of Father Christmas, he decided to drive up to his home.

On arrival, the cause of the delay became obvious. The old gentleman, dressed in his robes, was home alone, frantically waving at the window to draw attention to his normally friendly sheepdog. The dog was loose and promptly challenged his master and held him prisoner in his own home.

My father managed to calm the dog and chain him up, then all was clear to leave with his passenger.

Father Christmas arrived a little late, but was made very welcome by the children.

'WHAT THE DEVIL'S GOING ON?'

Rose Bindon, Penguin, Tasmania

I woke to the yowling chorus of an intense cat fight directly under the floor. A full, bright moon lit my bedroom.

My mother was already awake, having thrown open her bedroom window. I could hear her saying 'Scat, scat' in subdued tones, so as not to disturb the rest of the family. The yowling continued.

With firm, determined steps and muttering under her breath, Mother, in her nightie, jumped into her gumboots and stomped down under the house. Her presence still did not stop the racket. So, with fierce determination, she let the dog, Katie, off her chain and gave her the order of 'Scat 'em, girl!'

Now Katie was a very intelligent dog, but with an askance look on her face and a wag of her tail, she waited for the order to be repeated—which it was, this time with a note of anger. Katie knew that tone and it meant Mother was to be obeyed immediately.

Whether it was the noise from the fighting cats or she misunderstood Mother, Katie took off up the home paddock, through the bush and across a few more fields. Within half an hour (a record time) she had every one of the dairy cows, plus the cranky horse, rounded up and running down towards the cowshed ready for milking.

By this stage Mother was yelling 'Get in behind!' Katie was barking hard and fast. The horse was snorting and neighing and trying to get away from the officious dog. Cows were running and mooing. The cats fought on. Pandemonium!

Dad woke thundering, 'What the devil's going on!' The rest of the children sat up bright-eyed at the window, watching and listening.

At the sound of Dad's voice, the cats stopped fighting. Katie came to heel—Dad's heels. Mother stopped yelling and the cows stood quietly in the shed yard waiting patiently to be milked. Peace at last—at 3.30 in the morning! No doubt the butterfat was down that day.

MOBILE HOME

Peter Hall, Glen Alice, via Rylstone, New South Wales

Tan is a striking black and tan kelpie that grew from a very fearless pup and now, as a dog, just lives to be with the livestock on our mountain valley property.

He was whelped at a particularly droughty time, and my wife Vinny, like most women in the valley, had a few poddy lambs and a very inquisitive poddy heifer calf, named Daisy, to feed each day.

The poddies would line up for their milk at the garden gate and so would the pup, so that he could sneak a lick of the excess milk from a few faces and generally enjoy himself.

Consequently, Tan, due to the daily ritual of feeding the poddies, grew into a very knowing young dog that was very keen on still licking Daisy, even though she had grown to twenty times his size. They were great mates, and you would often see the big poddy heifer happily getting her motherly grooming from the dog.

This was soon to change though, for the young dog had started to get very keen with stock and soon had to be chained up, otherwise he would muster everything back to the house.

The heifer, on the other hand, due to the persistent drought and the knowledge that the hayshed in the house yard was the best place to be, especially if she was given the odd slice of bread by Vinny, was never going to leave. The heifer would lazily walk over to Tan to have a drink out of his water bowl, get a motherly lick and then wander off again. Why go to the stock trough for water when Tan was so obliging?

Then disaster struck and the friendship was broken up for ever. Daisy had gone to Tan's water one day when I was shearing a few sheep in the nearby shed. I had chained up Tan and he had drunk most of his water after mustering the mob earlier. Daisy was persistent and moved about sniffing at the bowl. Tan was also moving about her. In doing so, he tied the sweetest half hitch around her leg with his chain.

Suddenly there was an almighty bellow and bang. I looked up

from doing the long blow on my sheep and immediately ran to the door of the shed, the half-shorn sheep closely following me dragging its fleece.

In the tradition of a good 'Jolliffe' cartoon, there was the heifer, Tan and the kennel careering across the paddock. There I was trying to bulldog the panicking heifer, calling loudly to the wife to help me bloody well free my best dog from under her bloody animal.

Tan survived to be the best dog I had. However, for months after this incident he had the habit of taking his water bowl into his kennel.

MAINLY FOR ENTERTAINMENT

Graeme Hobbs, Kojonup, Western Australia

When I came home to work on the farm in 1962, two dogs, Laddie and Peter, were in residence. Laddie was a border collie and Peter was a black mongrel of indiscriminate heritage. Passable dogs working sheep, they were kept mainly for their entertainment value.

Laddie would ride on the back of the truck travelling seventeen miles from farm to farm, constantly snapping at the overhanging branches of trees, spitting out the mouthfuls of leaves while waiting for the next branch. One day he misjudged, grabbed a branch and was left swinging in the air as the truck passed underneath him.

Peter loved chasing sticks, balls and stones. When the occasional travelling salesman called, Peter would work on him for some play. Finding a rock or half a brick, he would drop it a foot or so away from the visitor's toe. If nothing happened he would pick it up and drop it closer... and so on until at last it would land right on the end of the toe, much to the consternation of several salesmen. It would depend on the opinion we had of the products being sold as to whether we would warn them or not.

BARKING ORDERS

Noel Drury, Hynam, South Australia

At shearing time, everyone is busy. Nobody has time to talk, relax— or even open their eyes.

The boss went off mustering sheep with Rusty, the red kelpie. They got to the mob in the back paddock and the boss sent Rusty around the sheep.

Now Rusty was a very erratic dog. Half the time he does what he wants and not what the boss wants.

Time was short and Rusty was being difficult. The boss was getting very annoyed and yelling at him. The sheep were going all over the place and still Rusty was racing through them completely ignoring the loud roars and somewhat colourful demands from the boss.

After some minutes, the boss turned away from the scene in disgust. To his astonishment, he discovered Rusty sitting behind him on the motorbike, looking a picture of innocence.

The boss turned back towards the sheep and, to his embarrassment, discovered he had been barking orders to a big, red fox!

FRONT-WHEEL DRIVE

Kay Hole, Naracoorte, South Australia

Joseph is a gentle man. He loves his dogs and they will do anything for him. He has a passion for well-bred kelpies.

On the particular day I am going to tell you about, he was determined to spend some time getting his new charge, Zach, working, even though Zach's front leg was in plaster. The exuberant pup would in time replace old, wise Sally.

The day was bright and sunny, although there was a chill in the air which comes with the first balmy days of autumn. The cattle first had to be fed, so the gentle farmer went down to the paddock with hay on the back of the ute and the two dogs in the front.

It was customary for Joseph to put the ute in gear, jump on the back and slowly feed out the hay while the vehicle bumped its way across the paddock. Zach and Sally were left in the front. Sally was there to protect the little pup and make him feel less frustrated. The windows were closed but not quite shut to the top, so that the dogs could manage to get air.

Contentedly, the farmer began to throw the hay to the bellowing cattle. Little Zach ran from side to side in the front of the ute so he could get a glimpse of his dear master. Sally was happy to sit and wait. All was right with her world.

Joseph collected the last bits of string from the wispy pieces of hay still left on the tray of the ute, then he jumped to the ground and grabbed the door handle on the driver's side. It wouldn't open. Zach was tonguing at the window—'I'm a good boy. I stayed inside with Sally.' Sally was looking a little dismayed.

After trying the door on the passenger's side with no success, Joe realised that Zach had locked each door with his little plastered leg. The ute was heading for the neighbour's fence and Joseph could be seen from all directions.

He decided to go down on his knees, making sure that he was not visible from the road (a man's pride was at stake), and try to turn the front wheels with his hands. It worked! But how was he going to stop the thing? 'Ah, the drain across the middle of the paddock,' he thought—'I've stalled her in that plenty of times before.'

The old Datsun responded to his now not so gentle hands and headed for the drain. Helplessly, Joseph watched as the old bomb casually crawled her way through the drain and up the other side without missing even one beat.

By this time, Sally was looking through the window and wondering why Joseph was using his 'rounding up the sheep' language just for a simple little jaunt in the paddock, and why he didn't get in and drive home. She was getting sick of all this.

She was not the only one. Joe had to quickly pretend he was leaning on the ute as it lamely wandered across the paddock, because the neighbour just then was travelling very slowly through one of his paddocks trying to see what on earth was going on. 'He's gone,' thought Joseph. 'Right, one more try in the drain.'

'Damn. Through again. Blast, I wish that pup would stop his infernal yelping,' Joseph mumbled as he front-wheel-steered the ute to a huge pile of logs. He quickly threw one under a back wheel, but it was too small and the old Datsun once more headed for the neighbour's fence.

Joe then summoned all the bits of strength he had left and grabbed a huge log, risking angina and hernia, to heave it under the back wheel. It worked. The ute stalled.

In the meantime, quite a few very slow moving vehicles were going at a snail's pace along the main road as their drivers watched this crazy farmer trying to steer in this novel fashion. What was the wacky fellow trying to do? There he was yelling at someone or something inside the ute, throwing logs at it and steering it from a kneeling position while it got perilously close to the road fence.

The pup's training was postponed until the next day and never again were the dogs left alone in the ute.

OH! WHAT A FEELING

Doug Keith, Elmhurst, Victoria

The tray of the Hilux ute was rusting away, mainly due to the male dogs using it as a urinal. So I purchased an aluminium tray as a replacement and put it into storage for the time being.

In due course, when there were no other urgent jobs, I parked the ute near the workshop and set about removing the old tray.

The dogs dozed in the sun, occasionally opening one eye to make sure that they weren't missing anything important, but generally conserving energy until there was some real action.

Eventually all the rusted bolts were undone and I removed the old tray from the chassis, and dragged it some twenty feet away. I then got into the cab chassis to go and collect the replacement tray.

Instant action from the dogs! Decisions to be made! In an instant, habit took over and all four dogs dashed for the old tray and leapt on. Oh! What a feeling!

But as I drove away, their euphoria evaporated and you could see their expressions change to—'Trust a bloody Toyota to fall in half just when we're needed!'

WHAT AM I BID?

Ralph Dawson, Birdwood, South Australia

During my 40 years as a stock agent in South Australia, I spent fourteen years at Angaston. Very often I was required to attend the

Gepps Cross sheep and lamb markets to assist in the drafting and penning of the various lots, and then to do some of the clerking of the sales.

I usually took my border collie Nimrod with me and he worked in the yards helping with the penning up. Often when we were selling, he would jump up on the walking plank above the pens and follow the agents along, watching the sales' progress.

On one occasion, he slipped past me and followed close behind the auctioneer. The auctioneer was taking bids from buyers in the race, and also from someone touching him on the leg. As bidding slowed, he glanced quickly down to see who was touching him, in readiness to knock the pen of lambs down to that person presumably in the pen below. Imagine his surprise to find that this person was Nimrod, rubbing his head against the auctioneer's leg. The eventual buyer was, of course, unaware that Nimrod had cost him several shillings due to his sham bids.

On the way home to Angaston, it was my unvarying custom to stop at a roadhouse just out of Gawler and buy two icecreams— one for myself and one for Nimrod.

YOU SILLY MUG

Arthur Finney, Broadbeach Waters, Queensland

It was early spring and as was usual I had risen at four-thirty. First thing was to send Patch, my faithful and ever-ready blue heeler, to round up the cows from the night paddock, driving them round to the yards for milking.

Meanwhile, I went back into the house for my usual early morning cuppa and piece of buttered bread. Coming down the back steps on my way to the yards, I looked over towards the night paddock.

It was still shrouded in a light mist. In the half light I could vaguely discern the outline of what looked like a cow that Patch had missed. 'I'll give that dog the rounds of the kitchen when I get to him,' I thought as I walked over to the yards.

Patch had the herd penned when I got to the yards. He was just sitting at the gate waiting for me to shut them in.

When I scolded him for leaving one of the cows behind, he seemed quite perplexed, looking at me in the quizzical way he did when uncertain of my wishes. He baulked three or four times at going back to the night paddock. Ultimately, I had to really bully and threaten him before, with a very sulky manner, he trotted off to bring in the cow that I reckoned he had missed.

Had I stopped to do the right thing, I would have had a quick head count. This would have saved me considerable later embarrassment, but being irate about the missing animal, I vented my impatience on Patch. I was certain I had seen a cow in the half light and morning fog.

There was no time to waste. Into the bails with the first six cows. Wash their udders and on with the machines. Get things moving, or I would be late for the milk carrier.

Then around the corner of the house fence appeared Patch, trailing, of all things, old Darkie. Darkie, my old draughthorse, was almost pensioned off and I had put him in the night paddock about a week earlier.

Patch slowly marched him to the yard gate. He then sat on his haunches and looked across at me with an expression on his face which seemed to say, 'There you are, you silly old mug, try and milk that one.'

RACING DOG

Barbara Shugg, Stratford, Victoria

We had heard of the oldest son borrowing Dad's car, and a younger son doing a bit of circle work around the front paddock, but were quite unprepared for the kelpie pup to take off in the farm ute.

It was towards the end of the '71 drought. The new black and tan was settling in nicely. He was showing plenty of eye and was very willing. The only command that he really understood, though, was 'sit'.

As was the daily procedure, the farm ute was loaded up with fifteen opened bags of oats. The young pup and the master climbed into the cabin and drove to the south paddock to feed the ewes.

The ute was put into low-range first gear and set in motion. The pup was left in the cabin while his master leapt onto the tray. Balanced precariously on the tail gate, he proceeded to trickle out the grain to the sheep, which were panicked into a feeding frenzy. The ute meandered slowly around the paddock for some distance and the frantic mob began to settle.

Suddenly, the motor roared. The ute bolted forward, sending the farmer flying off the back into the midst of his nervous sheep. The ute whizzed crazily around the paddock, bouncing in and out of potholes, scattering grain in all directions. The farmer and his sheep took off in hot pursuit.

The pup was of the 'when-in-doubt, sit' variety. The louder the boss yelled, the harder the terrified pup sat on the accelerator, the faster the ute bumped around the paddock and the more the bleating sheep panicked, chasing their food supply.

It wasn't until the farmer's voice ran out that the little dog ventured up onto the seat and peered out the window to see what was causing all the commotion. The boss, gasping gentle encouragement to the dog, finally managed to keep him off the floor long enough to catch his utility.

LOVED BY HIS OWNER AND NOBODY ELSE

Jenny Caldwell, Forbes, New South Wales

An old drover by the name of Mattie O'Connor gave me Wally as a pup. Wally was a little bit of kelpie and a lot of everything else. He grew up as most pups do, loved by his owner and nobody else—especially in my mother's garden and when trying to get the sheep through the gate.

Time went on and Wally thought he could do anything that was asked of him, so we packed a large chair and set off to a wether trial at Plevna, Trundle, New South Wales, which had yard dog trials on later in the day. Wally and I had never entered a trial before so this was a very brave move, more on my part than Wally's.

We were called to be eighth into the yards so we watched every move the others made, getting little tips on the fence from the veterans of this very male-dominated sport. The plan looked simple enough—fill the drenching race, then draft the mob three different ways and count them without physically helping your dog. Only verbal help and encouragement were allowed.

At this stage Wally, as you can imagine, was very hard to restrain as the excitement was all too much. There were dogs everywhere and I had quite a job to hold him. At this point I should add that Wally had a fetish for lifting his leg on every car tyre, every tree and every gatepost.

In the middle of the yards was a man who was to decide our fate, including whether Wally should be put to stud as a champion yard dog. There he was—crisp blue shirt, shiny riding boots and clean white moleskin trousers.

Our turn had come. The previous dog had been very well behaved and scored well. The bell rang to signal our start. I released Wally, and, well, he took off, jumped every fence, and was off behind utes and trees seeking other dogs. He had completely forgotten about the sheep. All thoughts of a blue ribbon vanished. The crowd loved this performance. The judge was not amused and

I was getting very embarrassed and thought, 'this is enough.' I called out, 'Walter.'

It did take a while but then I saw a brown blur heading towards me and thought, 'What a good, obedient dog.' Wally, however, thought he'd take a short cut via the judge, who at this stage was looking a little flushed.

In his excited state and with all eyes on him, how was Wally to know that those white moleskins were not another white gatepost?

Needless to say, Wally did not get a blue ribbon.

TEACHING THE APPRENTICE A LESSON

Neville Kajewski, Emerald, Queensland

My old friend Fred Wilson had a cattle dog called Ho, a wonderful worker and clever in many ways.

Ho wasn't just a good worker, he was Fred's mate and constant companion. I'm sure they knew each other's thoughts.

In the latter part of Ho's life, Fred bought a pup to train as a replacement before arthritis completely immobilised the old dog.

One day, Fred, Ho and the pup were yarding a mob of bullocks for dipping. According to established routine, once the mob was mustered Fred took the lead on his horse, allowing the dogs to bring them along while he opened the gates.

All was going well until a couple of bullocks decided they were going home. Under normal circumstances they would be no more than a nuisance to Ho. He would simply return them to mob with a couple of disciplinary nips to nose and heel, but he hadn't reckoned on the inexperience of the pup.

When the two bullocks broke away, the rest of the mob turned.

The pup, thinking he should be behind them, went to what was now the back of the mob.

Ho's barking at the two breakaways stirred the pup to enthusiastic action. At full pace he ran back and forth behind the mob, barking furiously and occasionally diving in to nip a heel for good measure.

Meanwhile, poor old Ho was working as hard as his arthritic joints would allow. Facing him was the whole mob, defiant and determined to escape. He blocked one then another group of breakaways, sending them back to the mob with tails high and nostrils flaring—but as he regrouped the mob on one wing, a breakaway started on the other.

Ho's exertions spurred the pup to even greater effort. The atmosphere became charged with the fear of confused bullocks being pushed around by the two dogs working in opposition.

Fred watched for a while, hoping the dogs would sort things out, but he finally decided to add to the confusion and help Ho while he shouted threats at the pup like, 'Come behind here, you bastard' or 'I'll shoot you'. He rode around the mob, cracking his whip, turning back one then another, but he knew failure was imminent. The bullocks had had enough.

Suddenly, cued by some primeval signal, the whole mob revolted. They scattered in all directions, making it impossible for dog or man to control them. Ho gave up. He knew he was defeated and let the mob go. It really wasn't their fault anyway... now, where's that pup?

As the bullocks streamed away around him, Ho ran straight for the pup who, with tongue lolling and tail wagging as he panted in the shade of a bush, was very pleased with his achievement. But the pleasure was short-lived. Old Ho wasn't at all amused.

He grabbed the pup by the scruff of the neck and shook him as he would a rabbit, at the same time scolding him for his stupidity with savage growls. The pup's yelps of fear changed to whimpers of submission. Ho dropped him but mauled some more warnings. Completely cowered, the pup rolled onto his back, baring his neck and belly, and awaited his fate.

Disgusted, Ho turned away from him, lifted his leg and peed on the bush, then trotted away to join Fred, whose laughter echoed around the ridges as they started again to muster the mob.

PART 7

OVER AND ABOVE
THE CALL OF DUTY

Going beyond the brief

A DEDICATED PARTNER

Geoffrey Blight, Narrogin, Western Australia

It was spring in the worst year of my life. I was broke. Sharefarming wheat was going very poorly and we were involved in a legal wrangle over the land and the house we lived in. My wife was pregnant with our first child, so I was glad to get some crutching on a local farm about nineteen miles away.

It was a small place, only one stand in the shearing shed, an old house, an old man and an old blue dog.

There weren't many sheep, about 1,100 all told, which needed crutching and then they were to be sold. The farm had already been sold and the old man was moving into a home in Perth. He had no family, just his dog and he was to be put down when the sheep were gone.

Scotty couldn't go to the new home—they wouldn't allow it and he did have trouble with his bowels and smelt quite often. Some mad young roustabout had run over him the year before as he sat by the shearing shed. I believe the old man had threatened to kill the young fellow if he ever showed his face there again.

The shearing shed was very old and rugged. A stiff breeze could have demolished it. It even looked as though it was ready to fly away. The shed only held about 50 sheep in just two pens separated by a picket garden gate. As I kicked off, the old man explained his predicament and also asked if I'd mind, each time I finished a sheep pen, throwing the picket gate open so the still unseen dog could do the penning up.

Well I had heard a few stories, I had been shearing for a few years and seen a fair bit of action, but I guess I didn't believe any dog was going to do what the old man reckoned. Still, he was a nice old fellow so I thought, if I had to, I wouldn't mind penning for myself. I'd had it worse. As the old chap wasn't able to stay for some reason or other, when I had finished the first pen, I did what he said. But I still couldn't see the dog.

I reckoned it was taking me about one and a quarter minutes to crutch each sheep. When I straightened up and saw the pen full, I received a shock as I had not heard any noise through the closed gate in the front wall of the pen.

When the second pen was done I repeated the exercise. Same result. I could hardly believe it. When I had the chance I directed a few how-are-you-mates to the bent old blue dog. He showed no interest in me whatsoever, even seemed suspicious of me, so I didn't push my luck.

The crutching lasted three days and was a piece of cake. The old dog had those sheep so well trained they penned more like milking cows than wild wheatbelt sheep.

I guess it was my praise for the old dog that made the old man ask if I would like old Scotty. He assured me that, although he could not run, he would still pull his weight for a while yet and as long as I didn't take him into the house, the smell wasn't too bad. He had visibly shown he wasn't looking forward to putting his dog down and no-one else wanted him. I thought he probably didn't know many people that well, having lived a very secluded life. The whole area had only recently seen extensive clearing, except for a few scattered properties, including his, that were the remnants of an attempt in the thirties to open up the land.

It was a few weeks later when the old man phoned and asked if I would come and take Scotty. He had to leave the next day. Scotty now became mine, but only till the next morning. By then, he was gone. I found him back at the now empty old house, looking pretty weary. That didn't stop him biting me as I tried, and finally succeeded in, pushing him into the car.

Next morning, I found he had slipped the collar and was gone again. I cursed him and swore he could go to hell.

After three days I relented. I took the gun and went back to the old man's former home, quite prepared to put him down rather than leave him to starve. He looked very old and hungry and surprised me by rising from where he had been sitting on the verandah and walking straight to the car, hopping in quite voluntarily.

Scotty didn't run away again but I didn't have much sheep work for him at that time so during the harvest, he just sat lazily around with our very useless labrador. They both passed their time killing hundreds of mice that were in plague proportion everywhere.

The harvest was a failure. By Christmas it was clear we would have to get out and go back to the sheep country I'd come from and go back shearing again.

I had about 600 mixed sheep running over 5,000 acres of sparsely cleared land on the cropping block where we lived. These would have to be mustered, which would take many days as they had spread all over the place in small mobs.

The weather was stinking hot, over 120 degrees on the back verandah of the tin shed type residence we lived in. I had thought I could probably catch the sheep at the three water points, though that would take even longer, building yards and shutting two points off. They might not even travel to the third water point anyway.

I was surprised when, just as the sun broke on Boxing Day, I became aware that a lot of sheep were bunching over some spilt wheat not too far from the house. It was a marvellous opportunity to just round them up and into the one yard we had. I was on foot with just Scotty, because it was too rough for a vehicle in most places, and I hadn't caught the horse. I sent the dog, fully expecting him to just pull them in.

As I have said, Scotty couldn't run and I soon realised that the sheep were going to get away despite my urging and swearing. Eventually, I hurled a stick at the dog, who wasn't going any faster than I was, which sure wasn't fast enough. Out of sight they went and I gave it up as a bad job and forgot about them.

The day was a real scorcher and there was no getting away from the heat. By mid-afternoon, the wife and I had settled for lying under the fan on the bed. I was nearly asleep when I became aware that large amounts of dust were drifting into the house, but we couldn't hear any vehicles approaching.

Staggering out the open front door, I was in no way prepared for what I saw. I had forgotten about the sheep and Scotty a good ten hours ago. I could not believe it. Here was what looked like 600 sheep moving very, very quietly and slowly up to the house, followed by a staggering, old, blue dog.

It was going to be a while before what had happened sank in. I swiftly took advantage of the muster and yarded them with total ease as the sheep seemed to quietly accept their capture. It was only when this was complete that I became concerned about the condition of Scotty—his staggering, his bleeding feet, his flanks tucked up and his fast and erratic panting. His eyes were sunken as he lay exhausted in the nearest shade.

In the next half hour I tried in vain to cool and calm and water him. It frightened me as he gulped and then shuddered in a fit as

I withdrew the water. However, greater powers than either of us took a hand. While I watched, believing that Scotty was very close to death, the wind came fast, followed by black storm-clouds bearing wonderfully cooling drops of rain.

Although the storm was short, it seemed to have the right effect. The dog lay motionless on the verandah, his breathing calm, and he now seemed able to cope.

Because of the rain, which is common to such hot climates, I had some trouble tracking what exactly had happened. It was obvious the old dog had continued that morning in his pursuit of the sheep, managing to keep them grouped to a north boundary for miles, before they had been turned and gradually pushed back. At times they would have had to pass through scrub and regrowth which would have presented any dog with trouble. He had probably seen no water at all.

Being then young, it would take me some years to realise the significance of that muster. As I worked and trained dogs I came to understand the incredible dedication that can be counted on in a dog when he has spent a lifetime sharing the job as a sole partner to a human being.

A DROVER'S MATE

Des Coombes, Coffs Harbour, New South Wales

Dan was a true drover's mate. I'm not sure how my father acquired Dan, whose parentage was never established, but many of the local experts reckoned he was a kelpie with a touch of barb in him. But there was no doubting his working ability.

My father often drove a mob of abattoirs bullocks from the Kempsey area and through the town of Macksville for slaughter, a distance of 50 kilometres. Dan was his only help. Without ever having to be told, Dan would block and direct the cattle in any problem areas along the way.

His reputation became so great that people would come out of their houses and shops in Macksville to watch Dan shepherd the stock through the town and over the bridge. If you know the town of Macksville you would realise how difficult the task was. Dan never missed a trouble spot or lost a bullock.

During the 1940s, when droving was the common way of moving mobs of cattle, a good cattle dog was a prized possession, especially when getting stock to abattoirs in a non-stressed state was paramount. On at least two occasions Dan was stolen, but each time an observant citizen would report to my father that he had seen Dan chained up at some farm in the district and Dan would be retrieved, happy to be back home.

My mother worked at a Kempsey cafe and often finished work late at night. When he wasn't away droving, Dan would lie on the doormat and wait to escort her home. He never was told to do this.

HOME DELIVERY

Madge Wilson, Clements Gap, South Australia

In the 1940s I lived near the railway line that went from Adelaide to Port Pirie. We used to have our daily paper, *The Advertiser*, thrown from the train by the guard at our gates in the paddock about a quarter mile away.

I used to carry my young border collie pup up with me to get the paper. As he grew I would give him the paper to carry back to the house. When he was older I started sending him to pick up the paper on his own.

Later, when he heard the train whistle which blew when it left the station, he would go off on his own, pick up the paper and deliver it to the back door. He did this for many years. He was a good sheepdog too, and was sadly missed when he died of old age.

SLEEPERS AWAKE

Patrick Boylan, Port Lincoln, South Australia

In 1937, my father was involved in a short-term contract as a drover with Goldsborough Mort. As well as his team of dogs, he employed the services of a workman named Charlie. Charlie's role was that of cook and camp-maker. Now Charlie, who was a model of virtue at first, soon showed signs of being a cupboard drinker. My father took it upon himself to ration the alcohol, but one particular day, Charlie, who was left behind to break camp, failed to catch up with the flock at the usual time.

Upon investigation, Charlie was located asleep in the horse-drawn cart. Closer scrutiny showed him to be very drunk and, despite every effort, he was unable to be roused. After some deliberation my father decided to assign his most reliable and loyal dog, Grundy, the task of looking after Charlie and the horse and cart. Grundy's lead was clipped to the horse's bridle and as the sheep moved along, my father would whistle up Grundy and Grundy would bring up the cart.

Later in the day my father's attention was drawn from Grundy and his role to the sheep. After a while, when he gave his usual whistle, no dog turned up.

After some searching he located the team. Grundy had gone up onto the railway line and the cart had become firmly settled between the rails. Being an intelligent dog, he had proceeded down the railway line. The continuous bumping of the cart as it went over the sleepers still failed to wake Charlie.

MAYHEM IN THE KITCHEN

Nancy Hyde, Port Lincoln, South Australia

Uley, the property where we lived when my children were little, was about 30 square miles of rough limestone country on lower Eyre Peninsula. The house was about 100 years old, thick-walled, with small, paned windows.

Apart from growing good wool, Uley was home to a great number of kangaroos, rabbits and foxes, which the dogs, both border collies and greyhounds, were encouraged to hunt.

One particular day, Brian and the family were out collecting firewood not far from the house. I heard a bit of a commotion outside but didn't take much notice, thinking that it was just another fowl being taken by a fox. I was very busy making biscuits for a Mothers and Babies Fete and concentrating on getting another trayful into the oven.

The next thing I knew, a fox with all the dogs after it came hurtling through the opening in the garden wall. The dogs were right on its tail and it didn't get a chance to turn. It just jumped onto the woodbox outside my kitchen window, then jumped straight through the closed window. It landed in the middle of my biscuits, showering everything with glass.

So, there was this fox in my biscuits on the bench staring at me a couple of feet away. I screamed and ran out the back door in search of Brian and the boys, who had seen all the fun and were shrieking with laughter—that is, until they got nearer the house and could hear the mayhem. The dogs had raced into the kitchen as I went out. We stood back and listened to the clanking of broken china and barking and general pandemonium. Then Brian summoned me in. 'The thing's dead,' he said.

I went in to survey chaos. China, biscuits and dogs everywhere and in the bathroom was the dead fox tangled in my bath towel. On the wall were its toenail marks where it had desperately tried to get out of the window. It had upset my face powder in the process, which just added to the rest of the mess.

The dogs stood around very pleased with themselves for good work well done!

BIRTH ON THE JOB

Joyce Shiner, Albany, Western Australia

Sissy was a young red cloud kelpie who was supposed to be chained up at shearing time, but somebody forgot. She was close to having pups and there were other dogs to do the work, so it was thought best that she was rested.

From the cookhouse window, I saw her drinking at the bowl under the tap, then she disappeared. Hearing a puppy yelping I went to investigate and found a pup in her bed. Several times she came back for a drink, each time leaving a pup or two. Then she would race back to the shed again.

At lunchtime we compared notes and discovered that Sissy had worked in the sheep yards all morning, returning to the house between jobs ostensibly for a drink.

The shearers were amazed to see her litter of newly born puppies, and she hadn't even missed a beat in the shed.

CHAMP, THE LONG DISTANCE LOVER

Richard L Mould, Naracoorte, South Australia

Nobody ever told us how Champ came to be on Lincoln Park Station, but it was clear from his intelligence, appearance and working ability that he was a particularly well-bred border collie. It was probable that he had been trained for sheepdog trials. However, he was too big and clumsy and he lacked the pace for a competition trial dog.

When handling sheep Champ could be controlled most successfully by whistles and hand signals alone, a routine foreign to our sheep station trained animals, who responded mostly to voice commands. On hearing a voice, in particular a raised voice, Champ would come straight to heel, and if the voice had any hint of menace in it, he would slink away. Indeed, he tended to be rather timid—far too timid for the rigour of sheep station work. This was in direct contrast to our mustering dogs, who were boisterous and somewhat rough and ready, not easily put down for long by voice or threat.

A good mustering dog is very fast and casts wide when heading a mob of sheep. Consequently the dog is quite often in the lead before the sheep realise it. Champ, on the other hand, tended to work too close, which meant that the sheep were being literally chased for a long time before being headed. This could have disastrous consequences if Champ became too tired to carry on or, as was his habit, to stop halfway to the lead and look for a hand signal. By the time he resumed the chase, the sheep would be over the horizon.

Mustering dogs had to be very tough, with a good constitution in order to withstand work day after day, week after week during the shearing, crutching or lamb marking seasons. In fact I had a black and tan dog called Whisky, who followed me for 70 miles in one day and he kept up with my horse the whole way. Champ, though, had tender paws, a soft constitution, and lacked the necessary stamina for mustering in large paddocks, some of which were over twenty square miles in area.

Our working dogs were short-haired kelpies or kelpie–collie crosses. But Champ, being a collie, had long hair which not only made him overheat in hot weather, but it also tended to pick up every kind of prickly vegetable matter imaginable. Therefore his coat would become a tangled mess of burrs and hair which, apart from hampering his movements, must have been very uncomfortable. To alleviate these problems, we periodically sheared Champ with the mulesing shears. After our dog shearing efforts he certainly did not look like a collie. Indeed, he only vaguely resembled a dog.

Since we used voices to control our mustering dogs, Champ would not work when other dogs were present. He had limited use as a mustering dog and he was useless for yard work because he could not tolerate large mobs of sheep at close quarters, yet he was brilliant when it came to putting a few sheep through a gate. This made us believe that he had been trained for trials rather than as an all-purpose working dog.

He was also very handy for carrying out the many station droving jobs such as taking shorn sheep away from the shearing shed, bringing mobs from outlying yards into the shearing or crutching sheds, and moving sheep when a watering point dried up. He was masterful at handling ewes with small lambs at foot. When a lamb breakaway looked like developing, he would crouch and stare at them. More often than not the lambs would decide that discretion was indeed the better part of valour, and they would turn and gallop back bleating to their mothers.

In fact he was so handy that we used to take him from Lincoln Park to Wartaka Station for shearing, crutching and lamb marking. Soon he was at home at either location. The two stations were 40 miles apart, half the journey being along Highway 1, which was mostly a gravel road in those days. This did not prevent Champ from making the 40-mile journey when a bitch came into season. If he was at Lincoln Park he used to make the journey to Wartaka. If he was at Wartaka he used to make the journey to Lincoln Park. How he knew when the bitches were in season from 40 miles away was a complete mystery to us.

We used to call Champ the Gentleman Dog because he always greeted us by sitting on his haunches, wagging his tail from side to side and extending his paw to shake. His manners when dealing with his handlers were similarly impeccable. But most of the time he kept to himself, avoiding trouble and keeping well out of the way of anything that might hurt him.

He avoided fights, but when cornered he would fight like a thrashing machine, and he won more scraps and sired more pups than any dog I have ever known. Indeed, Champ was a highly intelligent dog, adept at planning his moves and very adept at slipping his collar or breaking his chain when he needed freedom. In fact we had to tie him with an extra heavy chain and wide collar to control him.

When a bitch came into season on the other station, Champ used to plan his 40-mile trip to perfection. At some stage before chain-up time in the late afternoon, he would simply disappear. He would journey most of the night to the other station, when the temperature was cool and travelling was relatively comfortable. He would arrive at his destination in the early hours of the morning when his rivals were chained up. He could then carry out his courting free from interference by the other dogs.

One night my father and I were returning home from Snowtown sheep market. It was fairly late at night and we were still about twenty miles from Wartaka. Suddenly I caught the momentary gleam of a dog's eyes in the bushes. The presence of dogs running around in the bush always had to be investigated, so I reversed the utility and was about to swing around so the headlights would shine in the right direction to pick up the eyes again when suddenly I had an inspiration. I jumped out of the ute and called out, 'Here, Champ! Come on, boy! Come on, get up!' The command 'get up!' told our dogs they were about to get a ride and they would immediately jump into the back of the vehicle.

Next thing Champ came slinking out of the bushes doing his best to cover his stomach with gravel rash. He was on his way from Lincoln Park to Wartaka to do some courting and he knew he had been caught out and was in the wrong.

My father was all for making Champ run the remaining twenty miles. I protested, pointing out that somebody might pick him up and then we would lose him. It would be a more suitable punishment if we took him home to Wartaka and chained him up so that he could not carry out his courting. He would be so near to the object of his desires yet so far, and that would serve him right. My father agreed to this, and after chastising Champ for being a silly old fool to run 40 miles just to do some courting, we continued on our way.

When we arrived, my father grabbed Champ and chained him up before he could get anywhere near the bitch. It was Molly, my father's best working dog who was the centre of attention, and there was still time to lock her away before any damage could occur.

'I'll lock Molly up in the morning,' said my father. 'I can't have her in pup with shearing so close.'

Next morning when we went to work, who should be waiting at the garden gate but Champ. He had slipped his collar during the night and he greeted us by sitting on his haunches, with his paw extended, his tongue lolling from the side of his mouth, his tail wagging from side to side, and his eyes glistening. He looked extremely happy, which is more than I can say for my father. I was suddenly very glad that my father had chained Champ the night before and not delegated it to me.

Molly duly gave birth to her pups in the middle of shearing and the collie traits of her offspring were obvious.

Champ kept up his epic journeys for many years between Wartaka and Lincoln Park. Sometimes he no sooner made the trip in one direction than circumstances caused him to make a return trip in the other. Occasionally he forgot his manners and made the trip at shearing time. When this occurred his popularity was at zero level.

As for Molly, her litter of pups as a result of my father's inept chaining of Champ produced one of the best mustering dogs ever seen on the two sheep stations.

SANDY

Ian Burkinshaw, Benalla, Victoria

Tom McDermott was a drover and dealer who lived in Maldon, Victoria. He became known to me when I was a child during the 1930s through the dealings he had with my father, mainly buying and selling horses and hay.

Tom would often buy a mob of sheep and take them on the road (the long paddock) with Larry the van horse and Sandy. Sandy was a medium-sized dog, dark in colour, with sandy points. He always had his tail in the air.

The team had quite a reputation, especially in the potato growing districts of Bungaree, Newlyn and Dean, near Ballarat. It was on one of these trips that Sandy's ability stood out even more than usual.

Tom pulled in with the van and sheep to camp in a lane between two potato crops. There were only flimsy, three-barb fences on each side, not sufficient to keep sheep out. The cocky soon arrived on the scene.

'You can't camp here,' he said. 'Your sheep will clean all my potatoes out.'

Tom said, 'I'll give you a quid for every sheep found amongst your spuds in the morning.' A quid was a lot of money in those days, it could be equivalent to about $400 today.

The cocky was on the scene at daylight and to his amazement, not one sheep was amongst the spuds and it was obvious none had been in there during the night either.

Tom pointed to the little narrow track in the frost on the inside of the fences where Sandy had made his regular rounds during the night. Sandy's ability was such that Tom very seldom had another dog with him. The dog could handle 800 to 1,000 sheep quite capably on his own.

SOME DOGS HAVE TO DO IT

Peter Knight, Coonabarabran, New South Wales

It has only been in recent times that Hound has really found his niche in life. It came with the approach of Coonabarabran's annual show and the dog jumping competition. We decided to enter and do a bit of training, but Hound was absolutely hopeless. He just couldn't see any point to it and was not even the slightest bit interested in jumping over anything, unless it was a bitch.

The big day came and time for the big event. I was still caught up at the cattle shed tidying up the last of the Head Steward's jobs, cranky and stroppy as I am allowed to be for that one day. But off I went to make a fool of myself in the main arena. Hound was too busy shaping up to every other dog around to be the slightest bit interested in a stupid dog jumping competition.

The jump was starting to get quite high, but still Hound was more interested in fighting. As long as he was snapped back into reality for long enough to get him confused, we were fine. When I called him from the other side of the jump he just gave a hop and a skip over to the only familiar face he knew. Once we had worked out the psychology of the athlete in Hound, it was hardly a challenge.

Gradually, as the jump grew really big, the competition dropped off and there was less to sidetrack Hound. He actually started to realise what he was supposed to do—and, what's more, enjoy it. You could see he thought it was great fun showing off to everyone as he pranced around, tail high and adrenalin pumping. Besides, he had more attention from me than he had ever had. This was great fun, he reckoned.

I don't think we realised just what it takes out of a dog to be the top dog of Coonabarabran show. Hound pranced around for a bit with his blue ribbon round his neck. He offered a few cursory snarls to the other mere mortals, but you could see his heart was not in it. He made it to the bar with us while we had a celebratory drink but it was all he could do to lift his leg on the seating log and then curl up and go to sleep. He woke up in time to load the bulls at nine that night, then just slept in the passenger seat all the way home. Couldn't even raise a snarl at the trucks on the highway. It is a tough life but some dogs have to do it.

Hound was one of those dogs for whom the description 'man's best friend' was coined. A great mate, a lot of fun, just occasionally useful and a man wouldn't be without one for quids. He was just one of the many reasons that makes life so worth the pain that is often such a part of living in the bush.

They somehow make it worthwhile to put up with droughts one year then floods the next, prices as low as they can go one year then worse the next. Always there with a smile and never a complaint. May the Hounds of this world continue to help keep the sanity of Australia's rural folk. They work far better than any therapist.

BIRTH ON THE JOB NO. 2

Alan Werner, Jeparit, Victoria

Going back a few years I had a brown kelpie bitch called Snip. I also had a Willy's jeep that didn't have doors, which got me around the farm. Every time I started up the jeep, Snip would leap onto the front seat.

At one stage I had to shift a mob of sheep from one farm to another. Snip was very pregnant. After pushing the sheep along for a while, she hopped into the jeep, had a pup and hopped out again to go on with her job. After another few minutes, she hopped in again and had another, then hopped out again. She finished up having three pups on the front seat of the jeep during the trip.

Ten minutes after getting home and being put with her pups in the kennel, she produced another two pups.

That is what I call a good working dog.

PART 8

PULLING THE WOOL

- *Having a bit of fun*
- *Dogs using owners' weaknesses to advantage*

ONLY BRING TEN!

Les O'Brien, Alice Springs, Northern Territory

Like most blokes who run sheep, my dad always had a team of dogs to whom he devoted almost as much time and effort breeding and developing as he did to his sheep.

As in most teams the dogs were selected for particular skills such as mustering, yard work, shed work and even for something as simple as their ability to bark. This was desirable when he wanted a dog to keep the pressure on a mob to force it through the race while he worked at the other end of the race. Being a team, their collective talents contributed to getting the work done; but they didn't all work at once even if they wanted to. In order to keep them fresh until needed, they were generally kept tied up.

Dad had a particular dog named Mugsy that was good around the yards and OK for paddock work, so long as he had another dog to follow. If there wasn't a dog for him to follow, he would venture out only about 200 to 300 yards on his own.

One day an agent from the stock and station firm Pitt Son and Badgerys dropped in to inspect some wethers that Dad had in the house paddock. With the usual greetings and obligatory comments about the weather, they headed off to the shed to check out some paperwork.

The sheep were scattered around the paddock but a small group was relatively close by as Dad despatched Mugsy (the dog that just happened to be off the chain at the time). With a whistle and call of 'way back!', the dog sped off. As if it was an afterthought, he then called out, 'Only bring ten.'

When the men emerged from the shed a few minutes later, there was Mugsy with ten sheep bailed up in one of the open yards. Needless to say, the agent was more impressed with the dog than he was with the sheep.

Dad was still enjoying the joke, so he muttered something like, 'Yeah, but he's a bit slow. I don't know how many times I've shown him how to shut the bloody gate...'

'DIVIDE!'

Brian Richards, Port Pirie, South Australia

My story takes place in Two Wells, a small rural town about 40 kilometres north of Adelaide. It occurred early in the 1930s at the Two Wells Hotel.

A local farmer had acquired a new sheepdog and had spent considerable time and effort trying to train him to do his job. He proved to be pretty hopeless in spite of the efforts of his owner. His only 'skill' was to race straight through the middle of the flock of sheep then return to the feet of his master and look up in anticipation of some words of reward and a pat on the head.

One day the farmer had tied his trap to the hitching rail outside the Two Wells Hotel and left the dog sitting underneath whilst he entered to enjoy a 'couple' of drinks with his mates. Shortly after, an unknown farmer on his way home from the market at Gepps Cross, near Adelaide, called in to quench his thirst. He had noticed the kelpie sitting under the trap and had obviously been impressed with his looks.

After ordering a beer he struck up conversation with the patrons in the bar, enquiring as to who owned the dog outside. The owner spoke up and a conversation ensued about the possibility of the dog being for sale. The owner could sense a chance of making a few bob, which was pretty precious in that depressed era. He enthused about the dog to the stranger and after a price had been discussed the owner asked the prospective buyer if he would like a demonstration.

The other locals, having previously heard the tales of woe about the dog's lack of ability, also adjourned outside to watch the demonstration with great interest. There was quite a large mob of sheep in the paddock over the road and the two men and the dog wandered over and climbed through the fence, eagerly watched by the other men.

The owner sent the dog around, and at the appropriate time he waved his arm in the direction of the sheep and shouted, with great gusto, 'Divide'. The dog of course obeyed the command to the letter and the interested farmer was suitably impressed, quickly paid his

127

money and continued on his way. The locals returned to have another beer and a good chuckle.

THE BRAND READER

Alan Kettle, Bundaberg, Queensland

My story concerns a dog owned by a friend of mine, a dairy farmer with Jerseys, whose dairying country adjoined land grazed by Herefords.

My friend claimed his dog could read brands, and when the appropriate circumstances arose while visitors were on his property, he would demonstrate his dog's 'ability' with justifiable pride. The necessary circumstances occurred when some of his milkers would get through the fence and mingle with his neighbour's cattle. He would then set out to 'prove' his dog could read brands.

He would send his dog through the fence with instructions to bring in only cattle wearing his brand. The dog would then rush down and get in behind the mingled herd to drive them towards the home property. Every time, the milking cows would separate themselves from the beef cattle and head home, much to the surprise of the visitors.

Since the dog was of small build, he had to stand on his hind legs where the grass was taller to locate the cattle. This helped confirm the claim of 'brand reading' to the gullible friends.

Of course, the milkers, being anxious to get rid of their load of milk and always brought in twice daily by the dog, merely believed it was milking time when the dog appeared. Hence their trek towards the bails.

HEAVY OPPORTUNIST

Mrs J V Carey, Wilmington, South Australia

Since we live in the town, my husband has to travel to the farm each day, and he is always accompanied by our sheepdog Ace.

The dog is somewhat overweight and has to be lifted onto the utility each morning and lifted off at arrival at the farm. He would rather stay on the ute all day than get off by himself.

However, should my husband stop at the post office or shop and there are other dogs in the street, Ace can spring off, as nimble as you like, and join the other dogs. Marvellous, isn't it!!

UNDERSTANDING THE WORKING SHEEPDOG

Arthur Shepherd, Paringa, South Australia

During 1923, a Mr Pocock drove my grandparents to our farm in the South-East in a 1923 Dodge motor car. Each evening my father debated evolution with Mr Pocock.

One evening my dad told Mr Pocock that in the next 100 years, dogs would learn to talk, because at the moment they could certainly understand English. Mr Pocock reckoned that would never happen.

Dad said, 'In the morning I will prove to you that my sheepdog Boxer understands every word I say.'

Next morning, Dad took Mr Pocock to a spot near the woolshed where they could overlook a sixteen-acre paddock. Two of my brothers and myself went along to provide the audience. Dad gave a whistle and Boxer came and sat in front of Dad about six feet away, looking Dad straight in the face.

Dad said to Boxer, 'Just over there is a sixteen-acre paddock. Somewhere in the paddock there are about 30 sheep. They are usually in one of the corners. I want you to go along the western fence, keeping about one chain from the fence. If they are not in the north-western corner, go down to the north-eastern corner, round the sheep up and bring them along the eastern fence.

'When you get near the next corner, there are two red gum trees. If you want to, you may cock your leg on one of the trees. Then bring the sheep along the south fence and hold them in this corner just here.

'Now get on your way,' Dad said, and waved his arm in the direction of the sixteen-acre paddock.

Boxer made off at full gallop, jumped between the wires of the fence of the sixteen-acre paddock and proceeded to do exactly what Dad had told him. He found the sheep in the north-east corner, brought them along the eastern fence and paused to cock his leg on the red gum tree. (When this happened the audience jumped with excitement.) Boxer then brought the sheep along the southern fence to the corner near us and sat down and held them there.

Dad turned to talk to Mr Pocock, but he had gone, absolutely frustrated and beaten, and did not utter a word.

PS—Boxer, the black, white and tan sheepdog, had been doing this same routine at least once every two weeks for three years!

AMAZING THE UNINITIATED

Max Williams, Exford, Victoria

It was my daughter, with some of her first job money, who bought Ralph for me. I've had dogs before Ralph, and good ones too—but Ralph was really something special.

A pedigree border collie, from trials and working dog parents, he soon showed he could carry on the tradition of his forebears. The breeder, Vern Sullivan, was keen to see new blood in the trials circuit, and sent up a couple of his mates to encourage me. So every spare chance, Ralph and I, and three sheep, sometimes more, were out practising.

Now, my story isn't about Ralph's trials career, but his career does have a bearing on it. Rather, it is about what any sheepdog worth its salt does, and that's drafting sheep.

Our sheep agent came one morning to draft out some lambs from the ewes, a mob of about four hundred. As he was going on to a bigger job next, he had recruited a chap from the office to help for the day. This chap was a nice fellow, keen to get stuck into it, and had obviously seen somewhere that it was done by hopping into the pen, flapping your arms about, yelling 'Ho, ho, ho', and generally working up a sweat, while a kelpie springs on the sheeps' backs, barking furiously.

Well, we'd just started the job when, thinking to have a bit of fun, I said to this chap, 'No, we don't do it that way. Ralph is boss here. We'll just open and shut the gate for him.'

I could see he was a bit dubious, but I just opened the drafting pen gate, said to Ralph, 'Get over, Ralph,' and the yard was very quickly filled. Ralph then was in amongst them, pushing them through, no blocks and no barks, while we just chatted.

I could see the office chap was pretty impressed by this, so I thought I would jazz the next scene up a bit. As soon as the drafting yard was empty, I opened the gate again, and Ralph filled it up as usual. But now I played my trump card. Just as I was shutting the gate, I looked at Ralph and said, 'Ralph, I think we can get a few more in here. Bring another three.'

Now, I knew from my trials training that Ralph loved working three sheep, and that my chances of him bringing that many from the mob were pretty good. Sure enough, back he came, three sheep in front, and straight into the pen. If the chap was impressed before, then this time he was goggle-eyed.

The mood had grabbed me by this time, so while Ralph was in the pen pushing, I was saying things like, 'Steady on, Ralph, that's Karen and she's made a nice job of that lamb,' or 'Get that one there, Ralph, she's always been a smarty.'

On the next few penfuls, it was much the same. If I said, 'Get three more,' and Ralph came back with more, I'd just cover up by saying, 'OK, if you think they'll fit. You're the boss!'

All that was a long time ago now, and the agent later said that the chap couldn't stop talking about it back at the office—about how Ralph could even count.

Ralph is retired now. He's sixteen years old and his daughter does the sheep work. Ralph likes going shopping these days, so he can have the donut my wife buys him. He also likes lying in the sun.

When I first got Ralph, I said to my trials mates, 'Well, at least I know a bit about sheep,' and, 'This is what I'm going to teach Ralph...' Both statements were pretty stupid. I had much to learn about sheep, and Ralph taught me more than I taught him.

I know Ralph's time is getting short now and that one day he won't be with us. But in another way, he will always be there— over drafting sheep and amazing the uninitiated with what a real working dog can do.

RUBY AND THE TAILS

D Wight, Parkes, New South Wales

Mulesing time is usually a pretty bleak and depressing time of the year. Around the lamb cradles as you go about your job, your knees freeze and the wind whistles through the sheep yards. It usually rains, and everyone ends up getting covered in mud and blood. Hour after hour standing in the same spot doing the same repetitive job, we tend to run out of yarns and jokes, told to distract ourselves. There are some great talkers among mulesers and shearers. The more mundane, repetitive and unpleasant the job, the better the yarns.

Last year was no different from any other. Everyone was arguing about who was next to pick up lambs. It was freezing and the flow of talk had stopped because we'd been going for a few days and had no fresh stories to tell. All around us, lambs were bleating as they searched for their mothers and a drink. But when your spirits get low and things are at their worst, something often happens which sparks everyone into life.

Ruby was the most useless dog ever to step onto the place. She was destined for the bullet, but on this particular day, she'd been tied up in the back of the ute to keep her out of the way. Her continual jumping as she watched ewes and lambs eventually broke the chain. With that, the idiot dog bounded off the ute with the sort of delight that only a farm dog can fully express.

Grinning wildly, she raced around the paddock, came back, did a lap of the ute, jumped a few yard rails, then dived head first into the pile of lamb tails just to the right of the lamb cradles. She tossed them into the air, rubbed her head in them, then grabbed a huge mouthful and belted off across the wet paddock, ducking and weaving all over the place.

Now as you know, lamb tails are much more than the severed, pathetic little ends of lambs. They are the actual currency of a sheep station. They determine how much the muleser will get paid for his days of work. And for the manager, they are his guide to working out the lambing percentage to show how well his rams and ewes have bred. You certainly don't want some dumb dog leaping into the tails and stealing any.

So when Ruby did just that, the museler, Alan, dropped his shears and hurtled off after the dog. Everyone else stopped work and joined in on the chase too. Alan wasn't the sort of bloke who was built for speed, being round and fat. Nevertheless, he took off at top speed. The manager, the overseer and the jackeroo, who was me, followed. Ruby, after having watched all the other dogs working, and being tied up for so long, reckoned this was a good game.

She crouched, mouth stuffed full of tails and grinning. As we approached, she took off again, bounding wildly. As tails fell from her mouth, scattering all over the soggy paddock, Alan and the manager would make rugby dives for them and shove them into their pockets. It was pretty hilarious, but I didn't think it would be the right thing to laugh.

This stupid game went on for ages. Every time the dog had an empty mouth after scattering tails in the paddock, she would dive back into the pile, then exuberantly chuck tails into the air, before dashing off for more fun. Alan looked as if he would die from exhaustion—despite the rain that was falling, he was as red as a beetroot and really sweaty, as well as muddy and bloody.

Eventually we caught that stupid dog and tied her up again. We all had to comb the paddock for tails after work so the boss could count them and pay off the museler. Alan didn't reckon it was much fun being diddled by a dog. The work is tough enough, he says.

Anyway, that night the boss loaded up the gun to shoot the useless bitch, but she was lucky. One of his city friends arrived just as he was cocking the gun and offered to give her a home. She is now just a fat, lazy pet which is about all she was ever good for. But we often laugh about the day she tried to rob Alan of his pay. And it was a pretty good distraction too.

CHEEKY SINGER

Betty Draffen, Macarthur, Victoria

Cheeky, our kelpie-cross, had been unintentionally conditioned to sing a song on command.

Whenever my husband sharpened his combs and cutters on the grinder during shearing, the harsh sound aggravated the dog so much that he howled. Eventually he obliged with a 'song' without the accompanying noise of the grinder. All my husband had to say was, 'Sing a song, Cheeky,' and he would throw his head back and 'sing'.

One weekend Bill left Cheeky in the care of his shearers who were staying at the Jerilderie Hotel while he travelled home to Geelong for the weekend.

In the early hours of the morning the shearers stealthily took Cheeky up to their room and invited him to 'sing a song' to disturb another group of shearers with whom they had a score to settle. Cheeky's loud tenor voice disturbed them all right—as well as the publican.

I'm pleased to say it wasn't Cheeky who suffered any consequences. His friendly nature no doubt ensured that.

PART 9

ALL IN A DAY'S WORK

A SMALL BLACK OUTLAW
WITH AN HONEST HEART

Margaret Glendenning, Everton, Victoria

I am not sure where Dot came from. She just arrived. I was only a child and I welcomed her without hesitation into our family of animals and people.

Somehow, however, I gained the impression that she had been suddenly and desperately in need of a home, had been passed from hand to hand in search of one. There was something about her previous owners moving right away from the district in mysterious circumstances and with great haste. Such details didn't trouble my curiosity for long—it was not until later years that I began to wonder about her life before she came to live with us.

A small, black kelpie with alert brown eyes, she was not young. Polite, but slightly reserved at our first encounter, she settled in easily with us, though she ignored the hunting dogs. Dot proved to be a good paddock dog, and useful in the yards. She never barked—no use ordering her to 'push up' and 'speak up'. Still, she managed to get her woolly charges right where she wanted them, without uttering a sound.

The hidden talents of our new helpmate did not become apparent for some time. One late afternoon my father stood watching a large mob of sheep stream through the gate past him, heading for the open paddock. One of the animals caught his eye as it leaped upward to canter off towards the hills.

'Should have had a look at that one,' he said as he stepped forward and pointed to the rapidly retreating wether.

I had been idly watching Dot where she sat behind the fence rails. I saw her galvanise into instant full speed, shooting out under Dad's arm like a little bolt of black lightning. In no time at all the indicated sheep was back almost at our feet, unhurt, but on its side and helpless. Dot held on firmly with absolutely no intention of letting go.

I watched her in action many times after this demonstration. We only had to quietly say 'that one' and point. She never failed to bring her quarry silently and quickly to us. We used her to single out a 'killer' for the table or to capture an animal out of the mob that may have needed our attention.

A neighbour, watching her performance one day, laughed and slapped my father on the shoulder. 'Got yourself a duffer dog there, Jack!'

I didn't understand that remark. To me, a duffer was someone who unintentionally made errors, a bit of a bungler. Dot was no duffer—she didn't make mistakes. Her neat responses never wasted time or energy and I was sure she understood every word we said.

Time passed. Dot grew old and a little deaf. Like many aged dogs, she seemed to hear what she wanted to hear without any trouble. I was older, too. I knew now about 'duffer dogs'. I recalled how she would sit at dusk, tense, quivering with some unknown excitement, staring at the moon rising over the distant hills. Was she remembering happenings of her past life, or was I just inventing them for her? I could well imagine the scene. The vehicle furtively hidden in trees by the fence, the hushed whispers and shadowy figures. The barely heard, low whistle. An elusive dark wraith silently dropping sheep one by one, standing over them until they were collected. Another farmer complaining angrily after finding a dozen sheep missing when next he tallied his mob.

Dot slipped her collar one night. I doubt she knew what hit her on the nearby road. We missed our little duffer dog, our small black outlaw with the honest heart, and I was not the only one who cried.

WELL TRAPPED

Nigel Smith, Tamworth, New South Wales

In the 1950s and early 1960s my father was one of the best known drovers in the Southern Tablelands of New South Wales. His droving entourage consisted of a horse and sulky, a wagonette and draught-horse, an offsider (usually me or one of my brothers) and, most important of all, Baldy.

Baldy was one of the biggest border collies that ever graced the saleyards and his reputation as an exceptional working dog had spread far and wide. He was constantly called on to pass on his genetic code, from which Dad made good beer money.

When I was ten, Dad and I were droving a mob of sheep on the immediate outskirts of Goulburn. We were coming up to a T-junction on a main road. I suggested to Dad that one of us should go ahead to make sure the sheep went the right way. Dad said not to worry as the sheep had been that way a few times and knew where they were going. When the sheep turned the wrong way and started heading into the town, I didn't make any comment.

Dad was whistling and yelling for Baldy but he was nowhere to be seen. He made some very rude comments about Baldy and told me to cut through the paddock and bring the sheep back. They had by this time spotted the nice green feed that masquerades as house-holders' lawns and gardens, so there wasn't a lot of time to lose. I bolted over the fence and took off, dodging the briar and jumping the horehound.

Suddenly I had the triple sensations of falling, darkness and then immersion. I struggled for breath and grasped for something to cling to. What I found was warm and hairy with smelly breath.

Baldy and I were in that cold disused well for over two hours before we were rescued. Dad had spent those two hours rounding up the sheep from residents' backyards, no doubt cursing us both.

Baldy obviously had not had Dad's optimism and had judged the sheep would head in the wrong direction. He had taken off across the paddock only to fall through the rotten timber that had been used to cover the well. It was probably fortunate that I had fallen in too, otherwise we would never have found him.

On the other hand, I am not sure that I would be here today if he hadn't already been in there. He helped keep me afloat, warm and unafraid.

LETTER FROM MAURINE

Cecilia Howard, Clontarf, Queensland

The letters of my late sister-in-law Maurine Needham came to light when we were cleaning out the family home recently. In the late sixties, she was working on a sheep station in south-west Queensland and she wrote describing the dogs' routine.

... There are twenty-one sheepdogs on this station and they are tied up until 3 pm when the cook lets them go. When they see her coming, the din is unbelievable. They all start yelling and howling to 'let me off first'. Not that it makes any difference as they all trail after the cook until the last dog is free. By then she has twenty deliriously happy sheepdogs all over her as she tries to untie that last dog.

As soon as they are all free they go hell for leather through the yard and over to a medium-sized laundry tub which is always full of water. This tub holds four dogs—just. So in splash the first four and there they sit up to their chins in water and drink and drink. The other seventeen meanwhile are falling over each other round the edge of the tub trying to get their share of the water. Then out charge the first four over to the wood heap. Round and round the blocks of wood they go until they find a block to their liking and then do three widdles each.

In the meantime, the next lot hop in and for ten minutes or so there are dogs sitting in water, dogs drinking and dogs widdling—quite a humorous sight.

'I SHOULD BLOODY WELL THINK SO'

Marj Wood, Benalla, Victoria

One afternoon after a day's drenching up at the yards, we were putting the final mob of ewes away. They had to go through the small paddock next to the lane, across the lane and into a fresh paddock. So they wouldn't go charging off up the lane, the boss stood in the lane to direct them across.

'Keep the dogs with you,' he commanded as he went off to open the gate and stand in the lane.

Whenever we had Jo and Ben working together, they were very difficult to control as they kept trying to prove to each other how good they were, how rough and tough they could be and how much better each was than the other. Keeping them behind me I could feel them making little darting movements of escape, so I had to continually snap, 'Behind, Ben', 'Behind, Jo', 'Come beind', 'Behind!'.

The boss opened the gate and the ewes flowed across the lane and into their new paddock which was knee deep (on a sheep's leg) in green grass. (After eighteen months of terrible seasons this picture is but a distant memory!!)

Some ewes put their heads down and started eating immediately and others did happy little sproings through the gateway. Neglecting my duty, I was busy watching the sheep and not the dogs. The boss's irate shouting brought me back to the job in hand with a thud. Ben and Jo were behind the mob trying to put them through the gateway all at once and the poor ewes were getting rolled and bowled over in the dirt.

'What do you think you're doing, you =*#@¢#,' he shouted.

Ben and Jo immediately fell to the ground. The boss kept shouting. Genuine regret was the best policy I thought, so I fell to the ground too. Ben looked over his shoulder and saw I was getting into trouble, so he slunk back beside me and leant on me.

Noticing Ben was gone, Jo looked back and scurried over to join us, giving me a couple of quick slurps with her tongue in sympathy. The ewes slowly got to their feet, the dust settled and the final ewe went into the new paddock. The boss looked at the =*#@¢# who were all still in their 'we're very sorry' positions and shouted, 'Come behind!' Ben and Jo hurried to obey and I followed. We all sat at his feet looking very repentant.

'I should bloody well think so,' he said crossly, but then, unable to stop himself, started laughing.

'We're forgiven,' noted Ben, jumping about the boss. Seeing me still sitting there he nudged me with his nose. 'Come on, you can jump about now. He's not cross any more,' and he and Jo flung themselves about the boss, tails wagging and barking happily.

A LIGHT CASELOAD

Anne McLennan, Derby, Western Australia

The working dogs of the north deserve some recognition for their courage and character. They generally live shortened lives up here, what with all the hazards of their work and problems caused by living in the tropics.

Bodie was one of the funny old canine characters I knew. He was a blue heeler cross, mainly white in colour with blue spots. His short, thick neck and stout head were appropriate for his work with cattle, especially bulls.

He was a bit of a fighter too, probably encouraged by his young stockman–owner. A fighting/working dog is a status symbol among these cocky young men. Bodie's ears had that well-chewed look of a seasoned fighter—a bit like a boxer with cauliflower ears.

His owner, Ion, nicknamed Weevil, was head stockman at Mt House Station. He and Bodie were out in the stock camp at Spider

Bore. Each night Ion would tie the dog to his suitcase next to his swag, more as a gesture than a secure tether. It did the job and stopped him from going off scavenging or fighting.

That evening dingos were heard while the men ate their meal and discussed the next day's muster. As everyone settled into their swags for the night, tired after a long day's mustering, and with the fire beginning to die, Bodie became restless. Weevil, too tired to care what it was all about, drifted into a deep sleep.

Suddenly Bodie took off with suitcase in tow. A dingo had wandered into the camp looking for food. The poor old battered case with its halfhearted latches burst open, Weevil's clothes scattering everywhere. Bodie was oblivious to the now empty suitcase still bouncing and sliding wildly behind him. His only interest was in having a decent punch-up with the dingo.

He and the suitcase raced past the fire, which was now only a pile of glowing coals. As he did so, the suitcase knocked over the tin of petrol the cook used as firelighter. The petrol burst into a ball of flame ensuring everyone was awake. Some of the men had to leap from their swags to avoid the out-of-control case as Bodie continued his chase undaunted.

The dingo dived under the chuckwagon trailer and galloped out the other side. Bodie was in hot pursuit... until the case hooked around the wheel and pulled him to a tumbling halt.

Weevil reckoned he'd use another tether after that.

PRIDE'S SHORT CUT

Phillip Clerici, Sale, Victoria

During the 1930s my late father-in-law, Arthur Taylor, then proprietor of the Ensay Transport Service in far East Gippsland, had a kelpie cross named Pride. The dog had been a bit of a champion in his day.

One day Arthur and Pride unloaded a few sheep near the transport depot for transfer to the saleyards just around the corner.

The local pub, The Little River Inn, was en route to the saleyards, so Arthur popped in for a quick glass, leaving Pride to attend to the sheep.

Pride must have felt left out, because he directed the sheep through the front door of the pub and headed for the bar. However, the bar door was closed, so he continued with the sheep down the passage, through the hotel and out the back door. He continued on to the saleyards after his 'short cut' without losing any of his charges.

A TERRIER FOR DIRTY WORK

Brian May, Pine Creek, Northern Territory

Many years ago I had a small farm about five kilometres west of Pine Creek. I had a few buffalo cattle, geese, ducks, chooks, goats and a mob of pigs.

Once they had been fattened, I used to take about ten pigs each week to the abattoirs in Darwin in the back of my Toyota ute. I used to have to muster these pigs on foot to get them to a small holding pen from which they would go up a ramp and into the vehicle. It would take at least five hours to load these pigs on a Sunday afternoon.

It turned out that my wife wanted a small house dog—a fox terrier. We went to Darwin to get this dog. It was to be hers alone and I was given strict instructions that I was to have nothing to do with it. So I sat back and watched the little fellow grow up. My wife called him Panda because he had black patches over his eyes. When he was fully grown he stood about eighteen inches high.

Panda would always come up to me and whimper as though he wanted to go to work with me. One day I went off to load the pigs and Panda indicated he wanted to go with me, so I asked my wife if Panda could come.

At first she said no, but when I said I would keep him in the front of the ute and that he wouldn't get dirty, she agreed. We got to the paddock where the pigs were grazing. My son was with me as he was quicker on his feet. I backed the ute up to the loading ramp and wound the window down about eight inches so Panda would not get too hot.

Mustering the pigs on foot was exhausting. I could see Panda in the ute jumping up and down with excitement as we got the pigs closer. Next thing, out of the window came Panda. My heart just about stopped as I know and you know what a fair sized back-fatter pig can do to a dog, and I knew what my wife was going to do with me if anything happened to the dog.

Panda headed straight for the lead pig, grabbed him on the ear and steered him, with all the others following, straight into the pen, up the ramp and into the back of the ute. Panda was running up and down on their backs, barking and going completely mad. He loaded all the pigs onto the Toyota in ten minutes. I quickly grabbed him out of the pen. He was covered in dirt and pig manure and looked a real mess—but what a dog!

My wife went right off her head about his state but I managed to calm her down and eventually she let me use Panda every Sunday to load the pigs. I have seen a lot of working dogs over the years, but none with guts like this little one. What a worker—he saved me hours.

DON'T FORGET THE CHOOKS

Lloyd Collins, Nyngan, New South Wales

Shearing was in progress. During the midday break, my dog mustered the whole poultry mob of twelve hens and one rooster and took the chooks a distance of twenty chains to the shearing shed.

He was holding them at the sheep yards waiting for me and the shearing gang to return, presumably thinking we had overlooked them.

THE WRONG WHISTLER

Frank Condon, West Ryde, New South Wales

Bob was a good cattle dog. Whenever Dad whistled for the cows to be brought in for milking, Bob would do it.

We also had a pet rosella parrot named Joey who, like most parrots, liked to mimic things he heard. So, one clear moonlit night at about 3 am, Joey decided to mimic Dad's 'fetch the cattle' whistle. Bob, obeying what he thought was Dad's whistle, immediately began to round up the cattle.

The family was startled awake by drumming hooves and lowing cows, at a time when cows, like people, should be sleeping. Dad quickly called Bob off and proceeded to curse him.

It was only later when we heard Joey doing his new whistle that Dad realised he had misjudged Bob.

A WHIRLWIND AT
THEIR HEELS

David Griffiths, Port Lincoln, South Australia

When Mo first indicated his desire and ability to work in the sheep yards, I thought I had a freak. Then I discovered that Australian silky terriers have several original families and that they had been bred as working dogs. Mo proved that to be true.

During the latter years of my farming career, I owned three dogs—two paddock workers and the diminutive Mo. With a pedigree longer than him, he was eager to work and afraid of nothing. During drafting, after every 50 or 60 sheep he would come through the race to be sure I was there—checking I was doing my job as he was doing his.

Woe betide any ewe that doubted his authority and hammered him against the fence. With teethmarks on her nose, she would have a whirlwind nipping at her heels in the best blue heeler tradition.

At the end of the job Mo, dirty and often bruised, would be carried to the house to be cleaned up and praised. He was the best yard dog I ever had.

A CLERICAL ERROR

R H and H F Cherry, Armidale, New South Wales

We were droving a mob of sheep which had to be loaded on the train at the old Tamworth trucking yards. It was peak hour in the afternoon. We had traffic lined up on both sides of the sheep.

I had a little border collie bitch, a keen worker of whom I was very fond. I decided to let her off to give me a hand. Just as I did, a car overtook all the others and hit her. Seeing what had happened, my very irate husband cantered back on his horse swearing, abusing and calling the driver all sorts of names. The driver had his back to my husband because he was busy explaining his actions to me.

When he turned to face my husband, the cursing suddenly stopped. My husband's mouth fell open. A sudden look of shock replaced it, then just as quickly he said, 'Well, I don't care if you're Jesus Christ himself, you should be more careful.'

You see, the driver was a man of the cloth.

My dear little dog died of her injuries.

HOT TIPS FROM PEPPER

Pat Stewart, Helena Valley, Western Australia

My late husband ran a shearing shed to which thousands of sheep came for shearing for most of the year. The sheep were mostly big wethers for export to Kuwait. The pace for men and sheepdogs was very hectic.

Many fine sheepdogs worked for us, but one conspicuously stands out in memory—a black and white kelpie cross we aptly named 'Pepper'. He was an excellent yard dog and could also bring in a mob from the paddock with the minimum of fuss—two attributes that do not always go together, as sheep men will tell you.

However, Pepper had another string to his bow—he was an excellent dog trainer. We often had little pups coming on to learn the sheep business. Like a clever teacher, Pepper would show them by example just enough to learn, and yet give them sufficient scope for their natural instincts to be expressed. He would gently bite them if their misdemeanour was small, or yank them away if it was a significant error. If the learner was doing well, Pepper—at such times he always seemed to have a self-satisfied look on his face—would retire and watch placidly in the background. He was always watchful, though, in case his own talents were required again.

UP TO ME TO BRING IT OUT

Jim Kelly, Naracoorte, South Australia

I'm a miserable old sod who hates to spend money, so when some breeder offers for nothing a kelpie pup from working parents, I'm inclined to take the chance. I've had some considerable success too.

I sometimes think the owner is more important than the dog's pedigree.

My latest hand-me-down pup is now fifteen months old, and I'm at the stone-throwing, bad temper stage, when Chip's exuberant energy is almost more than I can handle, but, as from her first look at sheep a year ago, it's all there. The instinctive desire to work a flock or herd and the desire to please the boss. It's up to me to bring it out.

THE MASTER SPEAKS

Jean Birrell, Longueville, New South Wales

There was an old farmer down Bombala way who had the best sheepdogs in the district. No-one could come near them.

When asked how he did it, he said, 'Well, first you have to know more than the dogs.'

WITH AN EYE
ON THE CLOCK

Keith C Kidd, Youngtown, Tasmania

Every afternoon at 4.30, Bounce, my crossbred border collie, would find me where I was working out on the farm. He'd always go through a ritual of lying down with his four legs in the air for a scratch on his stomach. His joy would be almost too much for him to stand. The mood then would have to change and I would become stern and tell him to go way back and get the cows.

Away he would go flat-out, and half an hour later he would arrive back at the cowshed with the cows.

The mornings would be different. He would always take my neighbour's cows in first because he started milking at 4.30 am. He would then come home and have my cows in the cowshed at six-thirty.

This routine went on for years, through the whole milking season.

PART 10

TOUGH AND UNPRETENTIOUS

· *Unpampered 'real' dogs*

STRETCH GOES TO THE BIG SMOKE

Greg Standfield, Bourke, New South Wales

We were mustering bullocks for the next Dubbo sale on the flood plains of the Darling River just out of Bourke. As usual I had brought along my bold red and tan kelpie Stretch, usually a sheepdog, but quite capable of blocking up a mob of cattle.

We had the mob together when the lead started to head through a break in the fence and up an old irrigation channel, so I sent the dog to turn them back. He did so but in the process copped a kick in the hind leg from one of the 1,200-pound bullocks, breaking it badly about halfway down.

The local Department of Agriculture vet tried valiantly to set the break, but after a number of casts it appeared that the leg and joint would require pinning. As I was soon going to visit the folks in Sydney, where veterinary facilities are more advanced, the local vet suggested I take Stretch with me and have him attended to there.

We planned meanwhile to take Stretch to the local hospital, sling the radiographer a carton of beer and hold Stretch down on the X-ray table so that I only had to present the dog and the X-ray to the vet in Sydney and thereby save a few dollars (knowing how metropolitan vets charge).

So, off we headed to Sydney for a few days with the dog in the back of the ute. He seemed to enjoy the trip, with all the new scenery, but didn't go much on the traffic jam on Parramatta Road and decided to jump out (broken leg and all) and stretch the legs whilst the cars were pulled up. Other motorists looked somewhat surprised as he christened a few of their tyres and then jumped back into the ute.

After a day or so in Sydney, I decided to head to the vet's. A very flash clinic confronted us, neatly landscaped and painted very white. Nevertheless we headed in, me in my boardshorts and T-shirt (so as not to look too conspicuous) and my 'thinner than your average city dog' on the end of his eight-foot chain.

Well, talk about smell the gum leaves on us. We were on the end of some strange looks as we took our seat between a pure white Samoyed with an ingrown toenail and some other huge, overly pampered woolly dog called Heathcliffe, who was in to get his teeth cleaned.

As I was about to take my seat, one of the owners of these dogs commented on my 'nice looking country dog', which 'needs a feed'. Whilst acknowledging the compliment, Stretch went to the end of the chain and nonchalantly cocked his leg over all the *Women's Weeklies* neatly stacked on the coffee table near a settee. Obviously he was trying to convey some sort of a message to his pampered city cousins, but he certainly embarrassed me—not that I really wanted to read a magazine anyway.

After a short while the receptionist beckoned us to the counter. 'Name, please,' she said.

I replied with my name and address.

'No, no, not your name, the dog's name,' was her reply.

'Oh, his name's Stretch, but he's not real good at signing the cheque,' I replied.

With these formalities over we again took our seat, Stretch giving the other dogs a complimentary growl as we sat down.

Finally the vet came out to greet us.

'You don't want him to get away, do you?' he commented, looking at the rusty eight-foot chain attached to his worn leather collar.

'Oh, it's the only chain I've got,' was my response.

'We have little plastic leads at the door for you to use. Remember that next time,' he said, putting us quickly in our place.

Eventually, after the dog had to spend a day and a night at the veterinary hospital and me having to part with a large sum of money, Stretch was returned to me with the customary, 'Here's your Daddy come to pick you up.'

'Just give me the dog,' I said.

As we were leaving the surgery, walking past even more pampered hypochondriac pooches and numerous shelves containing dietary dog food for those canines with an obesity problem, I could imagine Stretch saying, 'Let's get out of this place.'

Footnote: Stretch with his mended leg soon after came second in the Open Yard Dog Trials at Brewarrina.

THE REVIVAL OF OLD JACK AT PAT RODDY'S PUB

Stan Harris, Wauchope, New South Wales

In early 1946, after losing the six best years of my young life with the RAAF in World War II, I realised I had to get started again to catch up; and also that I would need to work hard, so work hard I did.

I also realised I could not work for a boss, so with my knowledge of the meat trade, I took on a butcher's shop in Gulgong which was going at an almost give-away price—which was all that I could afford anyway. It wasn't long before I realised I needed a good working dog.

I had become friendly with Mr Charles Niven of Springridge Station, from whom I used to purchase fat lambs and who later was to prove a very good friend and mentor when the going became tough in the drought of 1946–47. During a yarn over a cup of tea in the shop, I asked Charles where I might find a good working dog.

'I have a good old dog out home,' he replied. 'He's now too old and slow for a long day's work and his heavy coat's too hot for him on hot days. I'll bring him in for you.'

The next day Charles arrived with the 'old' dog in his utility and presented him to me, giving him a pat on his head.

'He's a good dog and his name is Jack,' he said.

Jack charmed everyone with his personality. He also charmed me as a worker. He knew every trick there ever was to know with sheep, cattle and people. I think he could even tell the time. He would be at the slaughter yards when needed to yard up. He would be at the holding paddock before anyone arrived and would have the sheep in a corner, and at what seemed almost the same time be at the butcher shop to keep any stray dogs out of the backyard. He knew every word we said and a lot more.

Jack just loved to ride between the mudguard and the engine of our old 1939 Buick Coupe. Somehow he had psychic vision or

154

mental telepathy with me as he would be waiting in his position ready for me to move off even before I left the shop.

About fifteen months later, when the business had built up and I was almost too tired to continue, out of the blue I was made an excellent offer for the business at a huge capital gain which provided us with a wonderful 'bank' for our road back to prosperity. So we moved on for a short period to Gilgandra; and of course, Jack came too.

We left Gilgandra in late July 1947 with all our possessions in the old Buick, and Jack in his usual seat on the running board. We were on our way to Wellington.

There had been an enormous frost that morning. The sun was warm, but the wind was cold. About eight miles out of Wellington I looked down to see Jack and soon realised the poor old chap was frozen stiff. I stopped the car, took him in my arms and placed him in the front area with my wife and daughter, Colleen. They rubbed him and wrapped him up but he didn't seem to be coming round. We raced the old Buick to Wellington where I knew that at Pat Roddy's Railway Hotel there would be a big log fire in the bar.

When I took Jack in before the fire all the old hands—drovers, sheep and cattle station owners (it was sale day)—gathered around. One old chap said, 'I think you've lost your mate, soldier.'

Then someone else said, 'No, not yet. He just blinked his eye.'

A great whoop went up when Jack's front leg began to shake a little. What tremendous interest ensued as he gradually came to life, until finally he wagged his old tail and snuggled against me, with a look up to me that said, 'Thanks, boss, I'm OK again.'

Someone asked his name and I proudly replied that his name was Jack and that Charlie Niven had given him to me. Of course Charlie Niven was so well known throughout those areas that great yarns flowed about C A Niven and dogs during the drinking session that followed. Jack was toasted many times in hot rum and the merriment continued until it was too late for us to travel further, so we stayed at Pat Roddy's pub.

Jack spent the night in the garage with the old Buick, snug as could be in a corner which backed against the pub's donkey boiler, and the girls from the kitchen carried all the goodies out to feed him. What a charmer he was. What a day.

The next day we headed off for Coneac Station, owned by my wife's brother Hilton McCarthy. It was mustering time and Jack and I enjoyed helping out. When we moved on to Kempsey, we left Jack behind and he endeared himself to all at Coneac. A great number of good working dogs were bred from Jack and I think the breed has been established and continues even to this day.

Eventually Jack became really 'old' and stricken with arthritis (from the freezing at Wellington?). He died leaving us with many wonderful memories.

CAST IRON SOCKS

Des Richardson, Broken Hill, New South Wales

This is an amazing but true story about a border collie who has been working in and around shearing sheds in the West Darling area of New South Wales and Western District of Victoria.

The dog's name is Socks and he is owned by Mr A Norris, a shearing contractor, of Coleraine, Victoria. Socks is now ten years old. He had a pretty normal life up until he was about three years old. Then his adventures started.

He was tied up in the back of a ute outside a hotel in Coleraine when someone decided to take the ute for a joy ride. The ute was found three days later, parked on a beach just outside Portland. A woman noticed the ute on the beach. When it was still there the next day she notified the police. When the police arrived, they found Socks locked in the front.

When they opened the door of the ute, the poor chap jumped out and urine sprayed out of him everywhere. He was blown up like a balloon. The police couldn't smell or see any urine in the front of the ute. They reasoned he hadn't urinated for the three days he was locked in the front of the ute. They were amazed that a dog could go that long without urinating.

The next chapter of Socks's life was when he was about five years old. He was working at Devon Station between Broken Hill and Wilcannia. One day when he was walking through the engine room, a small child patted him which made him happy. He started wagging his tail, but the smile soon went off his face. He had got too close to the motor and his tail had got caught in the flywheel which spun him around a couple of times. He hit the cement floor on his way around and then his tail came off, leaving a stump of raw meat and bone about two inches long. When Socks realised what had happened he got up and went straight outside and started fighting with the nearest dog he could find—as if to blame him for the pain.

Socks was taken to a Broken Hill vet who cut off the stump and pulled skin over it. Now he looks a bit of a dag, especially when he is wet.

About two years ago, Socks fell off the ute between Broken Hill and Wentworth and was missing for eight or nine days before he was found at Kudgee Station, just off the main road. He had skin off him all over, his sores were infected and he had a dislocated hip. He took over four months to recover from that escapade.

This amazing old dog is still one of the best dogs working around the woolsheds that I have ever seen.

I'LL TEACH YOU A LESSON

E A Unger, Parkes, New South Wales

Nigger could claim no pedigree of any kind. However, between us we managed to do all the necessary work with my sheep in spite of his occasional mistakes.

In true public spirit I had ploughed a firebreak with a disc plough. This naturally left a furrow. To avoid thistles and grass I followed the furrow on my motorbike—with Nigger perched on the small platform behind the seat.

As inevitably happens when you are proceeding slowly, the front wheel fouled the edge of the furrow. Consequently I found myself flat on the ground and pinned by the bike.

Nigger, who had been thrown off, quickly summed up the situation. Before I had a chance to move, he lifted one leg and in true dog style, baptised me before slowly trotting off towards home.

I HAD GOT MYSELF
A BEAUTY

Shirley Joliffe, Mitchell, Queensland

I had been working in a newsagent's whilst my daughters were at school but as soon as they finished, I decided to return to the bush and mustering.

A young friend offered me his cattle dog, Ned. She was a medium-sized, cream and tan bitzer with kind brown eyes, floppy ears and dew claws as long as a parrot's beak.

At first Ned got in everybody's road when they were saddling up their horses by bringing sticks and stones in her mouth and dumping them at their feet. It wasn't a promising start.

The mob of cattle we had was stroppy. One broke away and I yelled, 'Fetch him back, Ned,' and she was off like a shot. Ned was a heeler and after a couple of death defying circles, the cow headed flat-out back to the mob—with Ned floating through the air like a trapeze artist on the brush of the cow's tail.

She came back puffing and wagging her tail. 'By cripes, you're a good dog, Ned,' I told her, realising I had got myself a beauty.

The cattle took some settling down, but we moved off with Ned looking anxiously for another breakaway. One of the boys cracked the whip and my quiet old horse nearly stood me on my head. The boys laughingly told me Ned had grabbed my horse by the hind leg when the whip cracked.

So came Ned's first hiding. I grabbed a switch. She cowered down, crawled over to me and took her punishment without a whimper. I gave her ears a tug telling her never to do that again and put down the switch. She promptly bent down, picked it up and proceeded to carry it along in her mouth, jogging beside me.

Ned always rode in the back of the truck with much glee. This day I heard a yelp and, stopping, found Ned getting up out of the dust with blood pouring from a cut over her eye and half her bottom lip hanging down. You'd swear she had just gone ten rounds with Cassius Clay.

'Cripes, Ned, you'll need cosmetic surgery for your looks, but we're miles from anywhere,' I told her.

She blinked at me through her bloodshot eyes and wagged her tail as if to say 'she'll be right, mate'. So Ned carried her dribbly lip for the rest of her life. Her head healed up fine.

I tried desperately to prevent Ned having puppies, but somehow she mostly outsmarted me. One day I went to fix a fence and when I came back to the truck, Ned was lying underneath it with one very dead, skinny little puppy.

'Ned, he's dead,' I said. 'We're going to have to leave him.'

She looked at me, picked the puppy up in her mouth and jumped up into the truck. She carried him faithfully in her mouth the 55 miles home. When I went to remove him, she clung on tightly for a while, then hung her head and let him go. Ned's old eyes watered. And so did mine.

LEFT IN A PIT

Stephen Vagg, Barmera, South Australia

An ex-livestock transport driver living at Burra in South Australia's mid-north walked from his house one day to find both of his kelpie dogs showing signs of having eaten snail bait, which had unfortunately been left lying around.

The old dog was near death. The younger pup, however, didn't appear to be so bad. On phoning the nearest vet at Clare, the owner was advised to bring the pup to the surgery immediately.

On the way, he briefly stopped at the saleyards and 'finished off' the old dog with a humane blow to the head with a large shifting spanner. He left him in a pit used for disposing of dead sheep. The pup was then taken on to the vet and, following treatment, duly recovered.

Twelve months or so later, while at the Burra sheep sales, the dog owner noticed a familiar-looking kelpie working sheep. He asked a fellow truck driver where he had acquired the dog.

It was revealed how the new owner had come across the dog about a year before, trying to extricate itself from the sheep pit in which it had been left, presumed dead. After the original owner explained the situation, the dog was returned to him, none the worse for the experience except for a permanent lump on the head.

Subsequent discussions with the vet indicated that the blow to the head may have saved the dog's life as during unconsciousness its system slowed, possibly providing better resistance to the poison.

STITCHED WITH STRING

Valda Farmer, Gawler, South Australia

During the Great Depression of the 1930s, my sister and I lived on a wheat farm twenty miles south of Bordertown, South Australia. We walked two miles to a little bush school at a siding called Wirrega. On the way we would always see dozens of kangaroos in the paddocks along the roadside eating the wheat crops. Unfortunately, the local cockies had to shoot them. Our father and his brother would ride out on horseback and, with the help of our kangaroo dog Bluey, would help round them up for the shooters.

On one occasion when Bluey had bailed up a huge six-foot old man kangaroo, he went in a bit too close. Before Dad had time to shoot the roo, the dog was slashed right down his stomach by the powerful back legs and claws of the roo, which was sitting right back on its tail.

Dad lay Bluey over the horse's rump and rode home as carefully as possible. When he got to the house we watched as he quickly found a big needle and string. After pushing Bluey's intestines back into place, he stitched the wound together. All this time Bluey didn't whimper or move. He just watched Dad with sad eyes.

We thought Bluey could never survive, but with loving care he did recover and once again ran with Dad and the horse after kangaroos.

A SYMBOL
OF OUR STRUGGLES

Patty Cahill, Moora, Western Australia

Bitchie never would have won a beauty contest. She was a rotund blue heeler with a sagging belly and spindly brown legs. But despite the massive proportions of her body, her head was refined, with a white star in the middle of her broad blue forehead.

Even as a young dog Bitchie was overweight, but it never stopped her from working. My husband Kym owned a station in the goldfields. Often times were tough and money was scarce. In desperation we'd drive around to the various windmills where the feral goats came in to water.

Bitchie would take a flying leap off the ute and get stuck into the fleeing goats. One day she caught thirteen, which was a record. Kym took the goats to town and the money he received for them was used to buy our groceries.

I still get shivers up my spine when I remember her bravery with the great white bull. He was a mammoth-sized Brahman cross, who'd run free all his life in the station country and never seen a human being before.

Earlier in the day we'd managed to throw the bull down and hobble him, but when we came back for him, he jumped up and charged towards our camp where the horses were tethered.

Kym let Bitchie go. Just as the white bull crashed into the yards, narrowly missing our horses with his massive horns, Bitchie latched onto his ear. He screamed in outrage and galloped away from the yards. Bitchie was flung repeatedly to the ground as the bull twisted his ugly head in anger, but she refused to loosen her grip. She managed to slow the bull down just enough so that we could get in close and rope him to the ground.

Her body was bruised and she limped for days afterwards, but at the time she was so proud of herself and sat down on her heavy haunches with a lopsided grin on her face.

Bitchie battled on with us, but later we sold the station and Bitchie retired. She got old and sick, but just before we were going to have her put down, she fell into an underground tank and drowned.

Bitchie was more than a dog to us. She was a symbol of our past history—our struggle to survive in the outback and our battle to keep ahead of bank managers and interest rates on the farm. She was a battler like us. When she died, a part of us was gone; a part that could never be recaptured.

SEARCHING FOR HIS TRUCK

Stephen Foott, Swan Hill, Victoria

The following is the true story of Butch, lost from a stock crate at Tailem Bend at 2 am one Friday morning.

Unaware that Butch had climbed through the bars of the crate, the driver returned to Swan Hill. All hell broke loose when it was discovered Butch was missing as he was a third generation truck and paddock dog.

I rang my brother, Peter Foott, who was working in Adelaide at the time. A day later Peter located Butch in the caravan park at Tailem Bend. Happy to be amongst friends again, Butch took up residence with Peter's family at Marleston, which is close to Adelaide airport.

But Butch was terrified of the sound of the jets taking off and landing. Returning home from work two days later, Peter discovered Butch had jumped over a six-foot galvanised iron fence and had disappeared. Peter rang the RSPCA and reported Butch missing. A search began and two hours later Butch was located ten miles from Peter's home, sitting in front of a service station apparently waiting for 'his' truck to come along.

After work one week later, Peter discovered Butch was gone again.

This time he had chewed his way through a flyscreen, got into the flat, smashed another flyscreen and escaped. Both windows had been open at the time. Peter rang the RSPCA, reported Butch missing and returned to Swan Hill for the long weekend. Sadness and disappointment prevailed and we gave up Butch as lost forever.

On his return to Adelaide, Peter once more rang the RSPCA. A terrified Butch had indeed been sighted running through the Adelaide traffic, but no-one had been able to apprehend him.

To Peter's amazement, three days later the RSPCA rang to inform him that Butch had turned up at the Noarlunga Abattoir, 27 miles from Adelaide. It was a location he had been to only three times. The last time had been two weeks previously, and wasn't via Adelaide, but over the punt at Wellington.

The drover at the abattoir had come to work early in the morning and found this red dog very tired and footsore at the gate. Immediately the gates were opened the dog had run to the truck ramps. The drover realised the dog was lost and rang the RSPCA.

Since his experiences in metropolitan Adelaide, Butch intends never to get left behind again, as he now sits beside the right-hand-side wheel of the truck after it is unloaded.

PART 11

NOTHING ELSE MATTERS

· *The job comes first*

IN THE HEAT OF THE NIGHT

Ian Waller, Beaufort, Victoria

I began my jackerooing in 1970 on a large property near Hay in the Riverina. I obtained my first working dog soon after arriving. It came with the name of Flea, because it was the runt of the litter. It was a small, hardy, black and white dog with impeccable breeding—out of Spec by Darky! She learnt her trade quickly and became a loyal and faithful friend. The name Flea, however, had a few variations— and it wasn't long before she answered to Fleabag and, later in life, Old Bag.

For two months during winter, a friend and I were at the out-station shearing shed living in the old shearers' quarters. Our job was to muster ewes and lambs for marking.

The hut that I slept in had a door that would never shut properly, so Fleabag was able to sneak in and sleep under my bed. To help keep out the cold on the frosty nights, I had borrowed a heavy jute woolpack from the shed. It was a very effective blanket despite the smell of wool and its weight. However, it turned out to be a bit too effective.

I started to notice that Fleabag's performance in the paddock was deteriorating. She was knocking up more quickly than I would normally expect. I could not work it out.

After discussing this with my friend who slept in the hut next door, all became clear. He told me the dog never got a chance to sleep. Because of the heat, weight and smell of the woolpack on me, I was having vivid sheep dreams. He could hear my commands of, 'Way back, Fleabag,' and piercing whistles throughout the night while I was fast asleep. The dog kept tearing out the door and barking way off in the distance trying to find the mob I was dreaming about. This was happening two or three times a night. No wonder the dog was worn out next day.

I decided to forgo the woolpack, so the dog could get a decent night's sleep.

STILL CIRCLING

J Griffiths, Beaumaris, Victoria

Bob's owner was Snow Anderson, who lived in the Terrinallum district of Victoria, which suffered a devastating fire about fourteen years ago.

Bob was well known and loved. He was reaching an age when some people thought he had run his time and could be put down.

On the morning of the fire, Snow told his wife he was going to move his stock—1,600 sheep and 200 cattle—onto a bare paddock. He took Bob to help him.

While they were there, the local fire brigade came by, called Snow over and told him a big burn was coming their way. Snow was an officer in the fire brigade, so he immediately climbed up onto the truck to help fight the fire. He didn't give Bob another thought.

While Snow was away at the fire, a wind shift turned the fire over Snow's farm. His wife and children knew what to do to save the homestead and surrounds.

The firefighters worked all day, then had the heartbreaking job of shooting injured animals, and securing what was left of the properties. Late in the day, Snow returned home exhausted. His wife persuaded him to have a meal before he went out to shoot his injured stock. Snow took his gun and set off to complete the tragic day.

When he reached the paddock, Snow found his old dog, Bob, still circling the sheep and cattle. They were all safe, but Bob had burnt the pads on his paws. Snow picked him up and took him home, where the family nursed him back to health and to live out his life to the full.

Sadly, this did not occur as Bob was hit by a car a few weeks later, but not killed. Snow and his wife nursed him again.

Three weeks later, Bob began to make an unusual bark. Snow said, 'I'll go and see what's troubling the old fellow.'

When Snow got to him, Bob crawled up on Snow's knee, nuzzled him and dropped dead.

Snow cried, and years later when we relate the story we still get a lump in our throat and tears in our eyes.

WORKING MOTHER

V T Mengler, Tenterden, Western Australia

Tootsie had about eight pups which, unfortunately for her, decided to appear just when our shearing began. As everyone knows, sheep-dogs are required to work very hard at shearing time, but with Tootsie facing motherhood, and then actually becoming a mother, she was put on 'maternity leave'.

For a few days she and the puppies were shut in their netted-in pen with kennel, food and water available. The puppies spent most of the time feeding or sleeping. However, this did not suit Tootsie. She heard the sheep and the men working in the yards, so on the first day her pen was opened for her to have a run, Tootsie worked out her own plan.

I was cooking in the kitchen but when I went to the back door I found that Tootsie had carried each pup about fifteen metres and placed it carefully on the back door step for me to babysit. She had already sped off to the shearing shed.

I put the pups back in the kennel, close together for warmth. As soon as lunchtime came, Tootsie dashed into her kennel, fed her brood, drank lots of water and was ready to go back with the men after lunch to work. She did the same at afternoon tea time and the routine continued for the rest of the shearing.

I always kept an eye on her pups in her absence.

A LUST FOR WORK

H J Treasure, Cowra, New South Wales

I have never known a dog enjoy his work so much. When it was over you felt like apologising to him. Choc had the look of a deflated balloon as he slunk away to his kennel to wait for the next job to begin. While waiting he always lay with his feet crossed like an old man. I don't know if this was body language for confidence or some other thing. But he always did it.

Choc could move across a sheep's back with the footwork of a dancer, or move under their bellies like a half-back breaking from the scrum base. He would use his front paws like hands, loading sheep. And as he grew older and stronger, he used his shoulders too.

Single out a sheep in the mob and he could catch it. His eyes would never leave the animal after he had singled it out. Find a lamb on the wrong side of a fence and he would stay there all day if necessary to guard it, belly low to the ground and eyes never off the face. Pick up a knife and sharpening stone and the killers would be under your feet in a few moments.

They say a dog is man's best friend. When things are going wrong as they sometimes do on the land, the dog often seems to sense it and stands as close to you as he can. Then he'll sit on your boot and lean against your leg to get a little closer. Somehow this always seems to make things a little easier.

DUTIFUL BLUEY

Anne Donovan, Wellington, New South Wales

Bluey, a blue heeler, grew up with our daughter Mary. When I put her in the sunshine in her pram, Bluey would station himself beside her and allow no-one and nothing to go near her.

As they grew older they were inseparable. One day I told her about Bluey and how he minded her in her pram. Unknown to me she took her dolls in their pram outside the gate and told Bluey, 'Mind my babies, Bluey.' She then went off and spent the afternoon about her business and forgot all about the dog and the dolls.

Later that evening at feeding time, Bluey was missing. Suddenly Mary remembered her dolls, and there was Bluey still on guard.

One day Mary and her dad rode into the saleyards with cattle. They left the horses and saddles in an unused stockyard, had lunch and then went to see the stock being sold.

During the sale we got a message that an interstate transport had got out of control at the creek and rolled at our gate. We hurried home to see what could be done to help. The horses and saddles ended up being left at the saleyards overnight. Next morning, Bluey was there—still on guard.

I'M NOT YOUR BLOODY DOG

Heather Edwards, Padthaway, South Australia

This is dedicated to pregnant wives who help in the sheep yards, where husbands turn into monsters—but quickly turn back into husbands once the job is done.

PARTNERS

I sit here in the protective shade assuming
   that soon my instant obedience to a command is looming.
I look and see just where the boss is now at
   is he scowling under that old felt colander-like hat?
Yes, his face *is* taut as his voice rasps out to me
   doesn't he notice my sad whimpering, my urgent plea?
Oh, for a rest for my time is not so very far away
   I should give birth soon, so please hurry on the day.

Yet faithful always and certainly eager to please
   I balloon forward into the mob with a certain unease.
My swollen belly hinders as my legs clip the top rail
   but I'm determined to yard these ewes and I will,
   I will avail!
So up the race I go with seemingly lightning speed
   but the boss thinks I'm slow and he's even more peeved.
I'm in the wrong place (again!) so I'm definitely told
   whatever happened to the days when I was worth my weight in gold?

Mingling dust and words scatter freely overhead
   I ache, heart pounding, with legs of jellied lead.
But the job must be done now and the drafting complete
   for the boss is always right and he must never be beat.
One stubborn old ewe with slaughter on her mind
   decides to block the race as a futile protest for her kind.
Blasphemies and hat fly high as he finally loses his cool
   and berates me more profusely as a useless, fumbling fool.

'That's it, I've had enough!' I want to scream.
  'I'm hot, dusty, tired and, yes probably useless in this team.'
Instead, silently simpering I snatch the toddler and flee the strife
And call back dejectedly, 'Remember, I'm not your bloody dog,
  I'm your wife!'

BOSS DOG

Alan Green, Mt Gambier, South Australia

Having worked as a wool classer throughout southern Australia for
many years, I have had the opportunity of seeing many great sheepdogs in action. The one that sticks in my mind was a beautiful dark
red-brown kelpie with a distinctive white ring around the butt of
his tail. He was aptly named Ringo.

In one particular shearing shed there was a race behind the
catching pens which was partitioned off with gates that slid up on
a counter balance, similar to a window. These gates were finely
balanced and could be slid up with a minimum of effort. Ringo
would go ahead of the sheep, put his nose under the bottom rung
of the gate, push it up, and then come back across the sheeps' backs
to force them forward. I am sure, had he been tall enough, he would
have pulled the gate down again.

Ringo's greatest act was filling the shearers' catching pens. As is
usual when the shearer's pen is down to one sheep, he calls out 'sheep
ho' to have the pen refilled. Ringo would appear flat-out as soon as
he heard the call and walk down the shearing board in front of the
catching pens until he came to the pen with one sheep. There he
would sit until the boss came to pen up.

If the boss didn't appear quickly enough, Ringo would find him,
grab his trouser cuff and give it a good shake. He would walk past

pens with two or more sheep and always propped at the pen with
one sheep. At times there would be two or more close calls of 'sheep
ho', and Ringo would always stop at the first pen with one sheep.
I never saw Ringo make a mistake in the six years I saw him work.

One of Ringo's greatest assets was that he would work for anyone.
His owner often lent him to growers to help with dipping, lamb
marking and so on. As soon as Ringo worked out the movement of
the sheep through the yards, which he learnt very quickly, there was
no need for orders or instructions. You just left it to Ringo.

By the way, for those who claim you spoil a sheepdog if you make
a pet of it, Ringo would sleep on the end of the boss's bed and always
travelled in the front of the ute. The best sheepdogs I ever saw were
those treated as pets and made part of the family.

BREAKING IN THE
NOVICE WIFE

Margaret Jones, Bathurst, New South Wales

Being relatively new to country life I thought it a novelty to put
on the gumboots and head for the hills to round up the sheep. My
job each day was to move them from an 80-acre paddock, and the
thrill of putting them through a double gate into the home paddock
to graze on the new oats was tremendous. At the end of the day
I had to move them out again.

After a couple of weeks of sometimes taking an hour or so each
time, and after the neighbours took pity on me and sent their dogs
over to help, we thought it about time to buy our own working dog.

We asked around and decided to talk to old Cliff, some 50 kilometres from home. Cliff showed us three dogs which he in turn put

to work with a whistle here, a word there or the wave of an arm. The decision was made. I asked the price of the rather scrawny, unattractive, plain brown dog that was our choice—'$300,' said Cliff.

My husband didn't blink an eyelid so I kicked him, mouthing, *Three hundred dollars,'* thinking he must have thought Cliff said thirty dollars. My husband told me to write out the cheque, which I found very hard to do for that boring-looking dog.

We took Sally home and all the time I was thinking what a huge waste of money it was.

Within the next week my life became very busy and moving the sheep twice a day became tiresome.

I would run past Sally sitting in her kennel on my way to pound the paddocks, thinking to myself, 'All that money for a dog and look at me, dirty, tired, cranky and totally unfeminine.' After another few days of this I couldn't go on any longer. I took the chance and took Sally with me, not knowing what to do or say to a fool of a dog. We walked to the top of the hill so we could see the sheep. I bent down and told Sally to bring them to me. As she disappeared over the hill I knew I had done a very stupid thing and that one of many unpleasant things was about to happen.

The dog would run away and there would go our $300. She would push the sheep through the fence to the neighbour's place, which would mean more money for repairs—or, worst of all, she would kill them. In my panic, I started towards home, not knowing what to do nor how I was going to tell my husband I had lost the new $300 dog.

When I turned back I saw the most beautiful sight. Six hundred sheep were heading straight for me with the most wonderful brown dog at their rear gently bringing them in. Still not knowing what to do, I ran in my gummies towards the gate and minutes later every last sheep was where it should have been with Sally standing there looking at me with her lovely big brown eyes. She had taken minutes to do what had been taking me hours.

I gave her a huge pat and much love and ran back to the house and rang my husband. 'Why didn't you give Cliff $600 for the dog?'

SORTING THEM OUT

Roy Postle, Pittsworth, Queensland

I was droving about 200 cattle from Toowoomba to Pittsworth when this event happened.

At a little place called Broxburn there is a watering point for travelling stock. The property either side of the stock route was owned by the Day brothers, who had a dairy and milked 45 to 50 cows. When I topped the rise, I saw that their dairy cows were just about home to the yards. However, two of my cows which had already had a drink were wandering off to join them.

I told Spot to get around them but they were in with the milkers before he could head them off. Without me telling him to do anything else, he went through the mob, found one cow and brought her out. Once clear of the milkers, a couple of good bites and she was on her way back where she belonged. Back he went again, and sure enough he did the same with the other cow.

While all this was going on, I was at least a quarter mile away, but the Day brothers were on the yard rails watching.

When I caught up to move the cattle on they called me over. They said if they had not seen what Spot had done they would never have believed it. And with a bit of a grin they asked if I would sell him. What would you think?

RELIABLE DART

Linda Irwin, Casino, New South Wales

Dart was a red kelpie owned by W J (Herb) Dunn and was descended from the first dog he brought to the far north coast of New South Wales in about 1910. There are thousands of kelpies up there now and most owners would claim they are descendants of Dart.

While Herb and Whispering Jack, an Aboriginal stockman, were asleep under a tarpaulin, their mob of 200 bullocks 'rushed'. Hearing the roaring noise, they mounted their horses bareback and galloped after them, hoping to eventually catch up and turn them. They were surprised to go only two kilometres before finding the panting bullocks and the dog standing quietly. Dart had gone, without direction, and turned them into a two-rail fence.

Herb often took mobs of cattle, mostly young or bullocks up to 1,000 head, through Casino with its many streets, lanes and empty blocks. He would steady the lead, and Dart, needing no instructions, would keep the mob moving by racing up one side, peering through the moving legs, and when the cattle broke away on the other side he would race around the tail and bring them together.

Herb often had to take cattle over the Richmond River at Coraki. He would notify the punt operator who in turn would warn travellers that the punt would be disrupted on a certain day.

One particular day Herb, with Hilary Lulham, a lad of sixteen, mustered 400 young steers and drove them to the landing area to get there just on daylight. Dart and 25 head were first on, and with a few whistles, Herb directed them to an area away from the punt landing. Each trip took half an hour. Dart met each load and kept the mob together without any further directions. The whole operation took ten hours and it was dark when the cattle were driven to a holding paddock.

SNIP THE RIDER

Gloria Godlonton, Bellingen, New South Wales

Snip was very active like his mother and took some controlling while young, so I commenced his training on a long lead. He proved to be a most intelligent animal, faithful companion and an excellent sheepdog.

He rode on the back of my horse even at the gallop. He moved to the front of me where I held him securely with one arm when the pace got really fast.

Out in the paddock when he was on foot he would put his paws onto my boot in the stirrup whenever we came to bindies or when he was getting weary after a long day. I would bend down and slip my fingers under his collar and he would leap onto the saddle blanket via my knee.

I always had to use a long saddle cloth as my mare Flight would not stand for the claws of his front paws. His hind legs on her rump did not seem to bother her after the first few rough rides Snip and I endured.

THE APPLE DOG

Stan Mentha, Mt Barker, Western Australia

In about 1955, we had around 1,500 sheep, but our main income came from an apple orchard. We exported about 5,000 cases of apples to the UK and the Continent annually, so the orchard and the fruit were very important to us.

We lived 60 kilometres from the sea and during summer we always liked to take the children to the beach at the weekends—but summer was when black cockatoos were a menace to orchardists. They would fly around in flocks of up to 200. Cockatoos will destroy apples at the rate of around one case per bird per hour, so in one hour, 200 cases of apples could be lost.

We trained our sheepdog Brandy to chase the cockatoos out of the orchard and he became so good that if a bird landed in the trees he would be there in a flash, barking and hunting it out immediately.

It was lovely being able to go to the beach knowing our fruit exports were safe. Brandy was worth many thousands of dollars to us.

SKIPPER

Kevin Clarke, Geraldton, Western Australia

This working dog story is about Skipper, a part border collie, bred by Sergeant Sanderson in Adelaide in 1960. Skip was my only dog and one of the few that I could draft ewes and lambs with single-handedly. This event happened on a sheep property I was overseeing south of Tintinara, South Australia.

We had prepared for crutching and were waiting for the team to arrive. Out of the blue, they turned up at 9 pm and asked if they could get under way at 7.30 the next morning. Obviously they couldn't, not without sheep in the shed.

I thought about it for a while and decided to night muster with Skip. I had a mob of about 500 four-tooth wethers reasonably close to the shed, so I tried for them.

I first drove the boundary and got the mob ringing. I then let Skip out with the usual command of 'fetch 'em up'. I drove well ahead, stopping occasionally to hear Skip barking when he turned the wings. Four gates and four paddocks later, we had them in the shearing shed yards. We pushed enough of a mob onto the grating inside the shed to start the first run in the morning.

Skipper was a brilliant one-man dog for both paddock and yard work. Although not good in the heat unlike the kelpies I owned later, he was patient with ewes and lambs and boisterous and fast with bare shorn wethers.

CHIPS WAS DOWN

Neil Finch, Balranald, New South Wales

It was two days before shearing and time to muster the big wethers about ten miles away in a paddock of some 8,000 acres covered in huge river red gums and thick spiky lignum bushes. Chips, my black and tan kelpie, and I got the sheep into a holding paddock in readiness to walk them to the yards the next day.

Next morning was cold, there had been a few points of rain overnight and the ground was slippery. Chips and I arrived at the yards in the old ute.

When Dad opened the gate of the holding yard, the sheep, for no apparent reason, took off wildly in all directions.

Quickly I jumped on my motorbike which we'd left at the yards overnight. Repeatedly kicking, I tried to start it. By this time the wetness from the seat had soaked through my jeans. I could see my companion standing by, the well-mannered dog that she is, waiting for the bike to start first before jumping aboard.

I tried again and again, continuously kicking, but to Chips's disappointment, the contraption still wouldn't start. I checked the choke and key, then kicked again, and suddenly the roar of the motor echoed through the tall gums. As soon as it started, Chips was on behind.

There was no time to warm up the motor. I pulled the stiff clutch lever in, slammed it into first gear, the chain gave a wrap and at high revs we took off, ripping up the sticky dirt and weaving in and out of the trees. As I found fourth gear, I realised I had lost my partner somewhere in the take-off. There was no time to go back and get her.

Jumping logs, crashing through lignum at full speed, I worked my way to the front of the mob. A clearing in the scrub was a help and I was gaining fast. But at that crucial moment, the chain came off, jammed and I came to a sudden sideways skidding halt.

I jumped off the bike and tried to head off the runaway woollies on foot, but my rickety knee couldn't keep up the pace and let me down. The sheep went running on. I raised my voice and loudly yelled words that most haven't heard before.

I gave up and turned to make my way back to my bike. Then a smirk came on my face. There was Chips, still coming along. This was my last chance. She went right on by me with one purpose in mind—just to head the mob. She gave me a cool, sideways glance as if to say, 'You wouldn't wait for me, so I don't need you.'

After already running close to a mile, her ears laid back, Chips, trying to run faster, really pushing herself, kept on going straight ahead. She knew where to go—my best mate, buddy, friend, my girl Chips. She rounded the sheep up and gained control of the mob in no time.

The wethers soon settled down and walked the miles that led on to the Sturt Highway where some travellers paid us the courtesy of slowing down for the sheep with a friendly wave. Many other idiots paid no attention to signs or travelling stock. Still, we reached the homestead sheep yards, and shearing was done with Chips, the all-rounder, continuing her great work in the shed as usual.

PART 12

A MIND
OF THEIR OWN

· *Doing it 'my' way*

A RATTLER ON THREE LEGS

Bill Donovan, Wellington, New South Wales

Old Jim was a drover with the best team of working dogs in the Back Country—that is, if you can take Jim's word for the fact.

'See old Biddy there,' said Jim. 'She's the best all-rounder I ever owned. Works wide in the paddock, jams 'em in the yard. Could put a bee in a pickle bottle.

'She's going to pup to Fred Scott's dog. Fred's dog is a fancy worker. Won a few dog trials too. Biddy has never thrown a bad pup yet.'

So I duly lined up a deal with Jim for the pick of Biddy's pups.

When the day arrived for me to take my choice of the litter of eight fat, grub-like creatures, I carried them a few metres from the kennel and placed them in a row. It has been ingrained into dogs from eons past to select the best pup first and take it back to the safety of its kennel—something to do with the survival of the fittest. Anyhow, the pup that I took home wasn't my choice, it was Biddy's. I've never known this method of selecting a pup to fail.

He grew up to be a playful nuisance, always in the wrong place at the wrong time with his tongue hanging out showing his teeth in a silly sort of grin as if he had a joke he would like to share.

The first time I took him around the sheep it was a freezing cold July day and he ran around puffing steam. One of my offspring said, 'You oughta call him Steamtrain, Dad.'

A man would feel a clown yelling, 'Go way back, Steamtrain,' so I compromised and called him Rattler, which suited him because he turned out to be a rattling good dog.

When he was being trained the property was infested with American burr grass (also known as spiny burr grass and many other names that I dare not write). It is a shocker on working dogs and Rattler got the habit of carrying one foot whether there was a burr in it or not.

One day a stock agent came out to inspect some sheep and after watching Rattler working them for a while he said, 'That dog would win at Molong Sheep Dog Trials. He has a lot of class, but you'd want to scrub him up a bit. You get points for appearance as well as working ability.'

I nominated Rattler for the Open Championship and took him to 'Le Fleur Dog Salon' to be spruced up. The young lady got me all flustered and nervous when she called me sir. The last time I was called sir was when I was pulled up for a roadside breath test on the way home after my mate's bucks party.

What with trying to explain that I wanted Rattler prepared for the dog trials and not knowing exactly what preparation was needed, I got her quite muddled. She kept looking at the dog and then at me as if she was comparing our IQs. By the look on her face as she ushered me out, the dog got top marks.

When I went back to collect Rattler, he was as shiny as a new billy can, toenails lacquered, teeth polished and—the most indignant treatment for any dog—shampooed. While I was leading that fancy looking hound out of the beauty parlour, I was wishing I was invisible. I felt like a police inspector sneaking out of a house of ill fame.

The trial ground was a hive of activity with the intercom drowning most other sounds. When Rattler's turn came, he performed like a true champion. Still displaying his old habit of carrying one paw, he finished the last turn and penned the sheep.

There was a pause on the intercom, then the request—'Would the owner of dog number 123 come to the secretary's office, please.'

When I arrived the head bloke said, 'I am sorry to inform you, sir, your dog has been disqualified because he's lame and we can't have lame dogs competing in sheepdog trials.'

I answered, 'He's not lame. That's a bad habit he got when I broke him in when the burrs were bad.'

The judge looked at me and said, 'This is my thirty-seventh year of supervising dog trials. I thought I had heard everything. Now you come along with a story like that. I tell you the dog's lame and I'd advise you to take him to a vet.'

It's annoying to tell the truth and not be believed, so I answered in my most indignant voice, 'He doesn't need a vet, he needs an animal psychiatrist to get him out of his bad habit.'

As I stormed out of the office, I overheard the remark, 'Someone needs a psychiatrist, but it's not the dog.'

HEAR! DOG!

Margaret Glendenning, Wangaratta, Victoria

Bluey's goin' deaf, ya know.
   Why, just the other day
I whistled him to block some sheep,
   He looked the other way.

Two hundred wethers charged the fence,
   Stampeded past the gate.
That dog just sat and stared at me
   Until it was too late!

He wagged his tail, and watched 'em go,
   They didn't stop until
They reached the scrubby cover
   On the far side of the hill.

Those sheep were wild as mad March hares,
   Long legged brutes, and cunning.
Don't know how he would've turned
     them,
   He'd have had to do some running.

Yesterday he got the cows,
   Came strolling in behind them.
The young bull wasn't with the herd,
   Way back, boy, go and find him.

(Jersey bred, and nasty,
   Don't trust him, stay on guard.
He hates all dogs and chases them
   On sight, across the yard.)

Blue ignored my signal,
   Looked positively dreamy.

Is he going blind as well?
    I'd swear he didn't see me.

I had to fetch the bull meself,
    I was careful not to cross him.
Last time he tangled with the dog
    He'd charged, and tried to toss him.

Poor old dog'll have to stay
    At home, take life at ease.
His biggest worry from now on,
    To shift to scratch his fleas.

Couldn't have him working stock,
    He'd be useless anyway.
I'll have to pension Bluey off
    To dream his life away.

Just look at the old codger go!
    He's jumped the garden gate.
You'd almost think he'd heard the scrape
    Of food fall in his plate!

School bus is early home today,
    The kids are loudly cheering.
Bluey's there to meet the boys—
    Too bad about his hearing!

WITH GREAT DISDAIN

Peggy Hodgson, Dalwallinu, Western Australia

Jock was trained very easily considering that he had four young children to untrain him and many distractions. One of his great strengths was his absolute love of sheep work. Once he learned to cast and take a flank, he wouldn't stop working. We had to tie him up or he'd be out rounding up any sheep he saw, whether ours or the neighbours'.

In his work, Jock was completely autocratic. He was a one-man dog who would occasionally and, with great disdain, condescend to work sheep for me. I had to learn my place though. He would allow me to drive him to the paddock and tell him what was wanted and then I had to shoot through. The moment I tried to drive a flank or help in any way, he'd turn the sheep the wrong way or push them through the wrong gate, just to show me who was boss. I suppose I could say we could work together... as long as I played twenty-ninth fiddle!

Left on his own, with instructions, he worked well for me, if somewhat distantly, but I always had to pick him up in the ute afterwards and bring him home according to his union rules.

My old father-in-law, who considered himself a good man with dogs, was helping us at shearing time and he took Jock out to the paddocks to help bring sheep up to the shed. Time lapsed and no sheep appeared. A search party was about to be launched when father-in-law showed up.

Shamefacedly he asked if someone could come and help him as —'That bloody Jock has boxed up all the sheep in the married couple's house yard and made a real Charley out of me!' He had too.

The boss did his quince and had it out with Jock. 'Get those bloody sheep out of there and up in the yards or I'll kick your backside!' he yelled.

Without so much as a cringe, Jock flew into action and the sheep were in the shed yards in no time. Like I say, he was a one-man dog.

PUTTING A DAMPENER ON THE DAY

Robert Pratten, West Dubbo, New South Wales

When leaving for work in the mornings in the Landrover, everyone would be keen and fresh for work. The dogs would hear the gate click and their chains would crash against the upturned iron scoops and drums which were their kennels.

Released from their chains they would rush off to soak the leg of the windlight tower or tennis court corner, then chase a couple of chooks and when I got into the Rover, they would leap into the back. Axes, sheep dip, tucker box and wire flew in all directions as they scrambled for a place.

Now Tiger, who did not like being the same as everyone else and who refused to copy what all the other dogs did, had been bounding all this time round my heels. So when I rested my arm along the side of the door to look back as I reversed (no rear vision mirror) I would feel a damp warmth spreading from my elbow and realise the horrible truth. Tiger had done in the back of the ute what he should have done earlier.

The only reason this dog ever survived was because he was friendly, faithful and would work, although mostly in the wrong place.

KEEP THE LANGUAGE PLEASANT, PLEASE

Wendy Muffet, Wirrinya, New South Wales

Wal, our border collie–kelpie cross, is one of nature's gentlemen. With his 'softly, softly' manner he has a deep-seated loathing of anything resembling roughneck colonial behaviour. He is always first choice when quiet handling is the order of the day, and so got the nod the morning we mustered the AI ewes.

All was going well until we hit the yards. We were on a fairly tight schedule and the boss was getting a bit frustrated with Wal's 'ever so gently' approach. 'For God's sake, Wal, *push 'em up!'* he bellowed.

Wal stopped in his tracks and looked back at us with a pained expression on his face, as if to say, 'I hope he's not going to start that ill-mannered yelling again.'

'Well, don't just stand there looking at us, you useless ****** !! Push those *bloody ewes up!'* roared the boss.

I don't know if it was the volume of delivery or the aspersions cast on Wal's family tree, but this poor behaviour simply could not be tolerated. He calmly padded over to the fence, jumped out of the yard and hopped up onto the nearby ute.

You can imagine the effect this act of mutiny had on the boss. With steam coming out of both ears, he told Wal loudly and explicitly (far too explicitly for the purposes of this yarn) what he thought of collies in general and Wal in particular.

Wal's response? He stood up, delicately turned his back on this tirade and sat back down again, gazing wistfully in the direction of the house yard where such 'paddock language' is not tolerated.

What could we do but laugh—and let one of the rough and tumble kelpies off to finish the job, leaving Wal to recover his bruised sensibilities?

THE EASY OPTION
LEFT DAD BOUNCING

Peter Waterhouse, Maya, Western Australia

About 30 years ago when I was a small boy, my father used to take me out kangaroo hunting with his two dogs Nip and Trixie.

It was too difficult to shoot kangaroos because we had a lot of regrowth bush on our farm, so he used kangaroo dogs instead. Those two dogs used to kill up to 80 roos a month, saving most of our crops in those hard times.

One Saturday afternoon the two dogs bailed up a boomer, well over six foot tall. My father decided to grab the tail of the roo to make it easier for the dogs to pull it down. Nip's neck had been stitched up a week earlier after being kicked by a roo, so by holding the tail, Dad hoped to make the dogs' task safer.

Just as Dad got hold of the huge roo, a smaller one hopped by. The dogs sized up Dad's roo and then looked again at the smaller one. They quickly decided to chase the smaller roo. This left Dad at the mercy of a very angry boomer which was keen to get hold of the creature hanging onto its tail.

Two hours later he was still holding on. After yelling for his dogs and bouncing around behind the boomer for all that time, he was exhausted.

His dogs returned wagging their tails as if nothing had happened. Dad couldn't afford to yell at them in case they took off again.

Eventually he persuaded the dogs to kill the boomer and he was able to fall back for a rest under the tree—that I had been up the whole time.

180 KILOMETRES AND ACROSS THE MURRAY

Joe Mack, Loxton, South Australia

Ginger was a nondescript, medium-sized mongrel (retired sheep-dog) belonging to an elderly couple in Barmera, in South Australia's Riverland.

His virtues were faithfulness and a placid nature. But his owners were old and growing feeble so, in the twilight of his life and amidst heartbreak, they gave Ginger to folk in Mildura, in the Sunraysia district some 180 kilometres distant.

Six weeks later, they were amazed to find Ginger, bedraggled, footsore and lean, at the back door! Enquiries revealed that his new owners knew of his disappearance, but had not wanted to alarm his previous owners by advising them, feeling somewhat guilty at not knowing what had happened to cause their new charge to vanish soon after arrival.

The whole story eventually unfolded, something like as follows. A truck driver used to commute regularly between the Riverland and Sunraysia districts and stay overnight with his lass at the Barmera Hotel.

He was travelling near Lake Cullulleraine, west of Mildura, when he stopped to study a brown dog in distress on the roadside. The dog responded by jumping into the truck through the open door, so the truckie watered the dog and drove on, wondering what to do with his companion, who was now quite contented.

On this particular journey, he had to detour via Loxton and then continue around Moorook, Kingston and Cobdogla before getting to Barmera. Between Pyap and New Residence (out of Loxton), the dog became agitated. The truckie stopped the truck, whereupon the dog headed for the nearby River Murray and vanished.

To reach Barmera from there, the dog had to swim the river and navigate through territory foreign to him.

SAGACIOUS LADDIE

Ken McCarthy, Heathcote, Victoria

This story about a brainy sheepdog from Daylesford appeared in the *McIvor Times*, Heathcote, Victoria, on 27 February 1890. It was reprinted from the Creswick *Advertiser*.

SAGACIOUS BRUTE

A remarkable instance of canine sagacity occurred at Kangaroo Hills on Friday last, the hero of the occasion being Messrs Tankard and Gordon's well-known sheepdog Laddie.

During the last two months Mr Gordon had been in the habit of taking at the end of each week a parcel of 60 or 70 sheep to a certain butcher in Daylesford. Last week however, he missed doing so, and the dog evidently thinking there was something wrong collected about 100 sheep from one of the neighbouring hills and set out with them himself, apparently for the usual destination.

Mr Gordon was away from home at the time, but returning an hour or two later, he missed the dog and the sheep.

Mrs Gordon remembered having seen the dog watching the sheep about the house at one time during the day, but did not know what had since become of them.

Proceeding on the road, however, Mr Gordon observed tracks of sheep going in the direction of Daylesford and following them up came upon the sheep about two miles from home, with the dog in charge—and conducting them—the day being hot and the sheep heavy—slowly along.

Laddie seemed delighted at the arrival of his master, but had to submit to being turned back.

Having given his orders, Mr Gordon returned home, and the sheep and dog followed in due course.

THIRSTY FELLOW

Beryl Parish, Stuarts Point, New South Wales

We had a cattle dog called Sam, a border collie-kelpie cross. He always followed my husband to the yard when he milked the house cow. My husband would always squirt some milk into an icecream container for the animals after he had enough for the household. Sam would have a drink and then the rest was brought to the house for the cat. When the container was empty it was left at the back gate for the next day.

One afternoon Sam must have got thirsty because I looked out the window and saw him pick up the container in his mouth and take it out to where the house cow was feeding and put it under her udder. Then he sat and waited, but she walked on after a few seconds. Not to be outdone, Sam picked up the container again, followed the cow and did the same thing. She didn't understand of course, and kept walking away until Sam gave up.

TARZAN THE SNAKE KILLER

Glenn Bradley, Bowraville, New South Wales

Tarzan was a ferocious snake killer. In the early days red-bellied black snakes were around in large numbers when there was much more timber and rubbish for them to hide in. Quite often they sought the sanctuary of the houses, so it was an asset to have a dog that would seek out and kill snakes.

On one occasion my father carried a load of wood into the house and threw it into the fireplace. Out crawled this big black snake, spitting and rearing straight at him. A hoe was handy and he chopped a hole in the floor killing the creature.

Tarzan would leap in, grab the snake behind the head, shake it viciously, release it, jump back and then leap in again, repeating the process until the snake was dead.

Death adders were also around in large numbers. They are sleepy, docile animals that will not get out of the way, but if you touch one they will flip over like a flash and you are history as they are deadliest of all.

Tarzan took a death adder one day, did not handle it quite so well and that was the end of him.

WITHOUT INSTRUCTIONS

Hilda Harkness, Esperance, Western Australia

When we were living in Langkoop, Victoria, some Department of Agriculture inspectors arrived on the farm to do a spot check for footrot and lice. The paddocks were too wet to travel in by utility, so the inspector and Woof were riding in the tandem trailer behind the tractor.

As we approached a mob of lambing ewes, Woof—without any instructions and to the amazement of all—leapt off the trailer, singled out and caught a ewe with lambing problems.

He was also very clever at picking out and catching flyblown sheep.

SCENTING THE WAY

Tom Robinson, Wilmington, South Australia

My dog story comes from an era when working dogs really earned their tucker. It was during the war years when petrol was rationed and prior to 'Ag' bikes. At that time, we had two female working dogs, sisters named Brownie and Kitty, and they never worked on the same side of a mob of sheep.

Dad and I were mustering various paddocks to get together fat lambs for railing to Gepps Cross market. Hammond was the railway siding at which we loaded and it was located in about the centre of our property.

Our first job on this particular day was to take a mob of sheep from a paddock six miles west of the siding. As we got them out on the road, one of the sheep wouldn't walk, so we loaded it into the back of the utility.

We left Brownie to take this mob of sheep to Hammond. We then drove to the railway yards, unloaded the sheep that wouldn't walk, and proceeded to another paddock that was located six miles east of the town to muster the sheep held there. Having completed this task, we then walked them towards the railway yards and were about one mile from Hammond when we met Brownie with her mob.

The local Postmaster at Hammond later told us that he saw Brownie bring her mob into the town, every now and then going ahead and smelling the ground to find the scent of our ute. In the middle of the town she turned the mob at the crossroads and detoured up to the railway yards (where we had unloaded the lame sheep) and not finding us there, again turned the mob and followed our tracks back through the town with the sheep, turned at the crossroads and proceeded on to meet us.

Nowadays, the increase in road traffic and public liability insurance risk would not allow such a feat as this to occur.

ANYONE SEEN ROVER?

John Griffin, Toorak Gardens, South Australia

My father farmed happily and desperately on the drought-haunted Willochra Plain in South Australia, from the late twenties till the end of 1949. Then, with the same sad lack of foresight which had marked our family's history on the land in Australia, he sold up in 1949 and moved south so that we could live closer to secondary schools. He wasn't to know that the Korean War was about to break out, sending wool prices through the ceiling.

Our sheepdogs were always locally bred kelpie-collie crosses. Good workers, intelligent, reliable and able to take their instructions from my father as he drove his yellow buckboard behind the sheep. We were a small operation with just one dog at a time.

We took our sheep for shearing to Boolcunda woolshed, north of Hammond. It was there, in 1948, that our dog mysteriously disappeared and we never saw him again.

Rover—the dogs were always Rover—was with us in the morning when we went to Boolcunda. The sheep had been driven there the previous day. When we packed up to go home that night, Rover was missing. He had been a reliable dog who always came home and we couldn't understand it.

Months later, the agents who handled our wool contacted us. Rover had been found in Japan—squashed flat in a bale of wool. It seems he had done a bit of adventuring in the old woolshed and had explored his way into the wool press. Rover gained some notoriety as the first dog from Hammond to travel to Japan.

However, the Japanese buyer, finding a flattened dead dog in his bale of reasonably good wool, had not been very pleased.

NOT SO USELESS

Bruce Mills, Tumby Bay, South Australia

Tiger was a black and tan kelpie owned by a family who lived in the rough hilly country of the Gawler Ranges. The two sons of the family were very competent motorcycle riders and rode their bikes over rocks and through scrub at a furious pace when mustering sheep.

Tiger was a large, heavy-boned dog and not suitable for carrying at speed on the petrol tank of a bike, so as soon as the going became rough he was pushed off and expected to follow. Now Tiger, being an intelligent animal, decided that if the boys were going to take all the exciting work he might as well go home—so he was branded as lazy and useless by his young masters.

It was shearing time at their station and I happened to visit. The father of the family suggested we go for a drive to check waters. It was a hot day and when we reached the tanks and yards we noticed about fifteen unshorn sheep a short distance from the trough. The sheep raced off and Tiger was sent after them and soon had them stopped. After giving them time to settle he walked in and started the sheep towards the yards, but at the first bush, one old ewe ducked underneath and stopped. The rest kept going. Tiger tried to fetch the old ewe out but she only shrank lower. Meanwhile the other sheep had curved off and were getting away.

Tiger left the ewe and turned the rest back only to see the old ewe take off in the opposite direction. Leaving the mob, he raced around the ewe once more, only to have her dive under another bush. This time Tiger showed his frustration and rushed under the bush at the ewe and she went right to ground.

Backing off, Tiger circled around the mob and drove them back to the ewe lying in the bush and waited and panted and all the time watched his sheep. After a while, the sheep mooched off and the old ewe got up and went with them. Tiger circled around them once more and guided them slowly back to the yards where he helped yard them.

So this is the useless, lazy dog, I thought. We had just witnessed some most intelligent work. Nine out of ten dogs would have either left the old ewe behind or stayed with it and let the rest go. Not only that, but Tiger's instinct to bring all the sheep to the ewe had overcome his training to bring the sheep to his master. He had in fact driven them directly away to collect the cunning old ewe.

BEYOND PRICE

David de Bomford, Forth, Tasmania

In the late 1920s my family lived on a farm on the old Surrey Road at Romaine, south of Burnie. My father owned a female border collie sheepdog which he had trained to drove sheep unaccompanied. On one occasion when he had bought sheep at the Cooee saleyard, my father sent them on their way and left the dog to take them home—a distance of about five miles.

My father had business to attend to and returned home via a different route. When the dog did not arrive with the sheep at the expected time, he went in search of them. He found them about halfway home and wondered why the dog had taken such a long time. An explanation was provided later by a local farmer who had seen the dog alone with the sheep and had watched her at work.

There had been a lame sheep in the flock and rather than hustle it along, the dog would allow it to have a spell at frequent intervals. She would let the rest of the sheep wander on but she was careful not to let them get too far ahead. She would bring them back to the lame one, gather it into the flock and urge it on a little bit further. Again and again she shepherded the sheep to and fro, all the while taking care to ensure that the lame sheep was given sufficient rest to allow it to continue.

Although the continual rounding up of the sheep and the back-tracking with them must have wearied the dog, her patience never flagged. Her efforts not only kept the flock intact but ensured that the lame sheep did not just make the journey, but did so with the minimum of discomfort.

The farmer was so impressed with the dog's capability that he offered to buy the dog for a substantial sum of money. My father would not sell her. She was beyond price.

PART 13

AT THE END
OF THEIR LIVES

GIFT TAKES ON THE JOB

Charles Vosper, Gympie, Queensland

The old dog was curled up in a ball. He was barely alive and shivering like hell. I don't mind telling you, tears came to my eyes when I saw him there. I knew old Darkie had moved his last cow in off the paddocks. As for the pup, Gift, I think he knew too, because he just lay there with his head resting on his front paws.

I told Peter about Darkie and he asked me to take him to the vet and have him put to sleep, but to bring him home and lay him to rest where he belongs. It was one chore I wasn't looking forward to, but it had to be done. After breakfast I found Gift was still there beside his old mate. He was a bit put out when I put Darkie in the truck.

That afternoon I let Gift off the chain, but he just didn't want to work. I had to get the herd in with some help from my wife. Gift had found the spot on the bank above the main yard where I had buried Darkie. He had a bit of a dig and sniff around it but wouldn't come away and leave him. He stayed there for three days, as if he was waiting for Darkie to get up.

On the fourth day I went down to the milking shed and had switched the lights on and was putting the rinse water through the machines when I had this feeling that something was watching me. There, standing in the half light, was Gift. He was crawling along down low on his belly and sort of crying. I took his head in my hands and said to him, 'I know, mate. I miss him too.'

You know, if I didn't know better I would reckon that dog knew what I said, for he seemed to liven up a bit. I gave him the order to 'go forward' and away he went. From that day on he never looked back. It was a real treat to watch that young dog working. The old dog had surely done a good job as a teacher.

THE EXPERT

Linda West, Wagin, Western Australia

There is always a power struggle between a farmer and his dog, but none more drawn out and obvious than that between Gus and Jim.

Gus was the runt of the litter, destined to rejection by everyone including his mother—until Jim decided to give him a go. Working on the assumption that he was used to having to struggle for everything he got, Jim thought this dog might just prove to be tough and tenacious. He was right. From the word go the struggle for supremacy between the two of them was a seesaw affair. Watching from the sidelines it was obvious that the dog thought he had won every round—and equally obvious that Jim thought he had. To the rest of the world it was plainly a rare thing—an equal working partnership between man and dog.

There was never any doubt that Gus was a star in paddock or yards, but at the house he was a problem, and the problem was his terrible appetite. He seemed to spend his entire life striving to get enough nourishment to make up for what was lost as a pup in the litter. He was extraordinarily clever at opening doors and jumping to great heights on slippery surfaces to steal anything edible lying around. Food was left out by a new, unsuspecting wife. Whole legs of mutton cooked and left to cool for the never-ending supply of cold meat disappeared from a closed kitchen.

Blame was sent flying around at all two-legged inhabitants of the house—accusations of tricks being played, tall stories of enormous blowflies carrying things away—until the greasy trail and paw prints were found. Gus again! He would open the kitchen door, jump up to the sink and drag his prize away to eat it amid the squashed area of garden reserved for his dining. Raw meat of course was a favourite and unloading groceries on a Friday afternoon had to be planned around the dog. Meat and other edibles first and all at once, or he would be in the car and off with a kilo of the best rump.

Gus was supposed to retire at twelve, but nobody told Gus. He continued ruling the roost and no other dog could topple him from his place. Everyone still depended on him but he did less running and more riding in the front of the ute. The young dogs were sent out to do the long stretches and he was called on for expertise and close work. He was beginning to lose his hearing and his sight, and arthritis had taken its grip on his back legs. Still he kept going. If the boss's boots and hat went on, Gus was still at his heels.

Gus retired himself at sixteen and took over the front verandah of the house. Every now and then as a mob of sheep went past he would wander out and scatter them to the four winds by being in the wrong place at the wrong time. The young dogs still gave him every respect and never challenged him. He was still top dog.

This was made obvious one day in the yards when two humans and three dogs were trying to funnel sheep through a gate. All was despair. The air was thick with dust and profanities, with sheep going everywhere and dogs becoming confused.

Through the dust, just in the nick of time, came the Expert, this time in the right place at the right time. The sight of him cheered the humans and galvanised the dogs into efficient action. He had sensed the confusion from his throne on the front verandah and had come to set us all to rights. He was very conscious of his own cleverness. We often caught him with a smirk on his face when he was proven correct. This was one of those times. Once he had sorted us out and had the sheep running through the gate, he took himself back to the house, pride and smugness in his every step.

AN OLD DOG RUMMAGING THROUGH HIS MEMORY

Paul 'Shakey' Brown, Mackay, Queensland

I sit here on a small beach. My memory wanders at leisure over the years looking for clues. An old man introducing his memoirs. No longer wearing a young man's clothes, I resemble more an old dog the family owned rather than an old man.

He was a cattle dog and, of course, they called him Blue. He was never brave but in his youth he had an amount of cunning. He displayed it when he saw a chained dog. Hair raised, ears back, he would race at the chained dog as if to do battle. The dog on the chain would prepare himself for the fray—bark, snarl, growl. Blue, having gauged the length of the chain, would stop his mad rush and casually urinate on a post barely out of reach of the other dog. Inevitably the dog would almost strangle himself on the chain trying to get at our heroic animal who would casually strut on his way.

However, Blue got older and in his dotage restricted his activities to our garage. Here the resemblance comes in. He devoted himself to searching out and stalking an unseen enemy. Every hair on his body raised, tail straight out behind, ears pricked, he would silently steal up on a garage pile of rubbish. On the first occasion he did it there was great excitement.

'Jeez', they shouted. 'Snake in the garage!'

Shovels were produced and the particular pile of rubbish was dismantled piece by piece. No snake. I think we did this a few times before we realised Blue was hunting the spectres of his own mind.

I was young then and believed in appeals to reason. I'd always respected Blue's intelligence so I set out to prove to him he was deluded. I would take apart each pile of rubbish he crept up on and show him it was nought but a pile of rubbish. This would satisfy him about that pile, but he would immediately begin to stalk another. And so it went on and on, and, because he was only a dog, and a senile dog at that, he'd return to piles we'd already investigated and stalk them again. So I had to admit defeat. Blue wouldn't admit defeat. He stalked the rubbish piles of that garage until the day he died. It was obvious from his effort and concentration that he expected each pile to render up the object of his hunt.

I'm Blue. My memories—his rubbish heaps. I sneak up on an event in memory, senses alert, expecting it to give a clue as to my predicament and meaning. I examine it carefully, then start again with undiminished enthusiasm. Expectations inevitably high. I'm a little smarter than Blue; certain rubbish piles of my memory I do not intend to examine again.

I don't know if Blue ever really knew what he was hunting. I know I'm searching for the reason I'm an old dog stalking the rubbish piles of his memory—often on chilly nights, when all the other dogs except the occasional adolescent are curled up in bed fast asleep.

A RUSTY OLD BLOKE

Joan Jackson, Warwick, Queensland

We named him Rusty but later found that his name was Tex. He arrived at our property very footsore, rheumy eyed, thin and very bedraggled. He appreciated a good feed and slept for a long time under the tank stand. A very tired old red dog.

We put ads over the radio and in the paper. Within a few days we heard his story. Since he had become too old to work the sheep on his home property, he was tied up while the younger dogs went out barking and bounding around, happy to be useful and able to do a day of mustering and yarding sheep.

Tex watched them—miserably whining and pulling on his chain, wanting to join them. His master decided to take the dog to his brother, who had also been 'put out to grass' and had a cottage 150 miles away. Tex stayed there two days and then left.

He found us 50 miles from where he started and when we looked at the map and drew a line from the cottage to our property and then to his original home, we found he was walking in a line as straight 'as the crow flies'.

When his owner contacted us through the ads we told him that Tex was settled and we all decided he would stay with us.

Although he had a reputation as a first class working dog, he never again looked at a sheep. He just slept in happy retirement in the sun. He seemed happy with his new name of Rusty, too—that is, until he became too deaf to answer to anything.

SLOWLY BUT SURELY

Judith Ridgway, Wolseley, South Australia

Old Purdie, our brown kelpie, had been on her last legs for a couple of years. She was fifteen years old with her hearing going, arthritis in legs that have covered many miles of paddocks and sheep yards, and lungs and heart not a hundred per cent. Despite all this she still managed to chase and bark at the washing trolley or lawn mower.

One particular day, four rogue sheep defied all attempts of the boss and young dog in the ute to get them to the yards. Then along came old Purdie, stumbling down the paddock. Slowly but surely she rounded them up, bringing them over to the boss to catch and load up. With head high, she rode home on the back of the ute with her catch.

Sadly she has died. We sat with her, talked to her and held her until that huge heart stopped beating. She was a friend and companion for half our married life.

She is still with us in spirit—buried at the top of the drive.

TO SAY GOODBYE

Mattie Allman, Sale, Victoria

Thirteen years ago my husband was given a brown kelpie pup and he named him Sim. A wonderful sheepdog, he loved every minute of his work and was very obedient.

My husband John retired two years ago but of course we kept Sim. The dog really missed his farm work.

One Tuesday in February this year, we were in the kitchen having morning tea. Sim amazed us by walking right into the kitchen. He had never been in the house before. He didn't seem distressed in any way and we wondered why he had come in.

Next morning my husband went out to let him off the chain. He found old Sim unconscious and he died two hours later. We think he must have come into the house to say 'goodbye'.

RETURNING THE PIGLETS

Kathy Cooper, Forbes, New South Wales

I recall vividly the day when Red had to fetch a litter of piglets through the gate to the correct side of the fence. Nothing unusual in that, perhaps, except Red was at that stage in the autumn of his life and almost totally blind.

He was a typical kidney-coloured kelpie who had worked in shearing sheds in western Queensland where my brother was shearing.

As he worked the piglets along the fence, it was difficult to tell that he had almost no sight. He would stop, cock his head, wait for a squeal or grunt from the main group of piglets, or a soft whistle from my father, then slowly advance on the squealing mob. Any breakaways from the main group were waited upon in silence until they returned, and then Red and Dad would recommence their job together.

Finally, when all the piglets were through the gate and relocated with the sow, Red just wagged his tail after a few rewarding words from Dad, who during the whole exercise had not moved one step from his spot near the gate, and had communicated his instructions to Red with soft whistles throughout the entire performance.

ENJOYING A LIFE OF INERTIA

Jennifer Hetherington, Grenfell, New South Wales

When our neighbour sold his farm to retire to the coast, he faced the dilemma of what to do with his faithful but blind old sheep-dog Tim.

We offered Tim a home and the company of our deaf old sheep-dog Bully. The veterans of paddock and sheep yard shared the house yard with a mutual indifference. Bully, a silent dog, did not intend abdicating or even sharing his role as boss and would deliberately ignore the newcomer. Tim in turn chose not to acknowledge Bully's position and constantly muttered to himself as he wobbled from one resting place to another.

Both enjoyed a life of inertia in selected spots of winter sunshine or in the reliable shade of the tank stand or vine-covered pergola in summer, living out their gentle retirement.

A BIBLIOGRAPHY OF
AUSTRALIAN
WORKING DOGS

Helen Hewson-Fruend, Gunning, New South Wales

FICTION OR FICTIONAL FACT

Baker, I, *Monday Sheepdog*, Angus & Robertson, Sydney, 1987. The story of the sheepdog, Charcoal, with his master in a range of farming adventures set in the imaginary district of Coonara.

Davison, F D, *Dusty: The Story of a Sheepdog*, Eye & Spottiswoode, London, 1947. The story set in Queensland of a kelpie–dingo cross.

Finger, C J, *A Dog at His Heel: The Story of Jock, an Australian Sheepdog*, John C Winston Co, Chicago, 1936. The story of an outstanding sheepdog, a crossbred Airedale Terrier, Jock, set in the late 1880s in Western Australia and South America.

Goode, A and Hayes, M, *Great Working Dog Stories*, ABC Enterprises, Sydney, 1990. A collection of previously unpublished stories about predominantly South Australian working dogs.

Lamond, H G, *Towser the Sheep Dog*, Faber & Faber, London, 1955. The story of a sheepdog, probably kelpie, set in western Queensland.

McGuire, F M, *Three and Ma Kelpie*, Longmans, Green & Co, Croydon, 1964. A story based on fact set on a sheep station near Broken Hill. Ma Kelpie had three pups, but their owner and one of the pups were lost in the bush.

Patchett, M E, *Ajax the Warrior*, Penguin, Harmondsworth, 1953. Ajax was a wild dog rescued from a flood and raised on a cattle station on the Queensland-New South Wales border. Ajax was the canine protagonist in other Patchett stories: *Ajax: Golden Dog of the Australian Bush; The Call of the Bush; The Golden Wolf; Ajax and the Haunted Mountain;* and *Ajax and the Drovers*. All have been translated into several languages.

Pollard, J (ed.), *Wild Dogs, Working Dogs, Pedigrees and Pets*, Lansdowne Press, Melbourne, 1968. Reprinted in 1977 as *Great Dog Stories of*

Australia and New Zealand, Rigby, Adelaide. A collection of previously published stories and poems about dogs from the preceding 100 years. It includes several Henry Lawson dog stories and poems.

Webb, Z V, *The Shared Dog*, Georgian House, Melbourne, 1945. Originally published in the *Bulletin*. The story of Spot, a mongrel belonging to two swagmen probably during the 1930s Depression.

Willey, K, *Joe Brown's Dog Bluey*, Rigby, Adelaide, 1978. A story of a blue heeler cattle dog set in desert country in central Australia.

Wrightson, P, *Moondark*, Hutchinson, Melbourne, 1987. The story of an Australian cattle dog, set probably in Queensland.

TECHNICAL BOOKS

General

Brown, J G (compiler), *Dogs of Australia*, KCC of Victoria, 1973, 1984.

Hamilton-Wilkes, M, *Kelpie and Cattle Dog*, Angus & Robertson, Sydney, 1967, 1980, 1982.

Kaleski, R, *Australian Barkers and Biters*, New South Wales Bookstall Co, Sydney, 1914, 1933. Facsimile edition, Endeavour Press, Sydney, 1987.

Sanderson, A, *The Complete Book of Australian Dogs*, Currawong, Milson's Point, 1981, 1987, 1988.

Cattle Dogs

Redhead, C, *The Good Looking Australian*, Readhead, Adelaide, 1979.

Robinson, N, *Australian Cattle Dogs*, TFH, Neptune City, 1990.

Sheepdogs

Border Collie

Bray, J, *The Border Checkpoint*, Bray, Mittagong, 1989.

Moore, J, *The Canine King*, Standard Newspapers, Cheltenham, 1929.

Vidler, P, *The Border Collie in Australasia*, Gotrah, Kellyville, 1983.

Kelpie

Austin, T and Zaadstra, P, *Our Australian Kelpie*, High Thunder, Mt Gambier, 1991.

Brody, J, *The Australian Kelpie*, Brody, Holbrook, 1980.

Donelan, M, *The Australian Kelpie*, Donelan, Wagga Wagga, 1982.

MacLeod, N, *The Australian Kelpie Handbook*, MacLeod, Altona, 1984.

Parsons, A, *The Working Kelpie*, Nelson, Melbourne, 1986, republished as *The Australian Kelpie. The Essential Guide to the Australian Working Dog*, Penguin, 1992.

Sloane, S, *Australian Kelpies*, TFH, Neptune City, 1990.

TRAINING, BREEDING AND CARE

Austin, T, *Breeding and Training Sheepdogs*, Austin, Coleraine, 1978.

Cavanagh, R, *Australian Sheepdogs*, Cavanagh, Whittlesea, 1990.

Dookie Agricultural College, *Dog Handling Workshop*, Victorian Department of Agriculture, Melbourne, 1981.

Glenormiston Agricultural College, *Working Sheep with Dogs*, Victorian Department of Agriculture, Melbourne, 1981.

Greenwood, G (ed.), *Farm Dogs*, Australian Government Publishing Service, Canberra, 1979.

Kelley, R B, *Animal Breeding and the Maintenance and Training of Sheepdogs*, Angus & Robertson, Sydney, 1942. Reprinted as *Sheepdogs, Their Breeding, Maintenance and Training*, 1949, 1958, 1970.

Lithgow, S, *Training and Working Dogs*, University of Queensland Press, Brisbane, 1987, 1988, 1989, 1991.

Parsons, A, *Training the Working Kelpie*, Viking O'Neil, Melbourne, 1990.

Russell, D W, *Managing the Sheep Dog*, South Australian Department of Agriculture, Adelaide, 1975.

Victorian Department of Agriculture, *The Working Dog*, Victorian Department of Agriculture, Melbourne, 1977.

GLOSSARY

Ag bike   agricutural motorbike, a tough machine specially designed for farm use.

AI   Artificial Insemination or artificially inseminated.

back   verb. describes what a dog does when it runs over the backs of sheep to push them forward as in a race, pen or yard.

bindies   bindi-eye, a native grass with unpleasant prickles—usually Calotis hispidula.

blue   noun. a blue heeler

chain gave a wrap   what happens to a slack chain on an old motorbike when it misses a few sprockets before taking hold.

cloud   dog's coat of reddish colour flecked with white

cockies   grain growers and cockatoos.

coolie   working dog usually with flecked coat and wall eyes believed to be bred from a German strain of working dog.

dinkum   real, genuine

growers   producers of anything off the land, eg wool, meat, grain.

hanging one on him   to punch him

header   grain harvesting machine

heeler   dog which nips livestock on the back of the hind legs to make them move forward.

jumbuck   sheep

Merle   dog's coat that is blue or red and intermingled with white flecks

mules   to cut strips of skin from breech area of lambs to prevent fly-strike. Named after J H W Mules who pioneered the procedure.

pickled, as in wheat   treated with fungicide and pesticide.

poddy   hand-reared calf or lamb, usually due to death of mother.

quid   a pound. Currency before 1966. Then worth $2.

race   a narrow, fenced passage for drafting sheep or cattle.

red cloud   a strain of working dog originating from the WA dog Red Cloud, bred by King and McLeod, or from King and McLeod bred parentage. Red Cloud was a big, all red dog of outstanding ability. His name was used to describe his descendants as in the case of the original Kelpie.

shave off a break   to prevent an animal breaking away from the mob.

tail   the back of a mustered mob of animals

'the more you ate, the better you were paid'   A drover's pay includes keep, so it stands to reason that they are being paid more if they eat more.

tonguing   panting with the tongue hanging out.

windlight   wind driven power generator usually 32 volts.

wing   either side of a mustered mob of livestock